TRAVELLERS

BEIJING
& NORTHERN CHINA

By
GEORGE McDONALD

Written by George McDonald, updated by Peter Holmshaw
Original photography by Alex Kouprianoff and David Henley/CPA Media

Published by Thomas Cook Publishing
A division of Thomas Cook Tour Operations Limited
Company registration no 1450464 England
The Thomas Cook Business Park, 9 Coningsby Road,
Peterborough PE3 8SB, United Kingdom
Email: books@thomascook.com, Tel: + 44 (0) 1733 416477
www.thomascookpublishing.com

Produced by Cambridge Publishing Management Limited
Burr Elm Court, Main Street, Caldecote CB23 7NU

ISBN: 978-1-84157-946-7

Series Editor: Maisie Fitzpatrick
Production/DTP: Steven Collins

Printed and bound in Italy by Printer Trento

Cover photography: Front L–R: © Yang Liu/Corbis; © World Pictures/Photoshot; © Dallas and John Heaton/Corbis
Back L–R: © Da Ros Luca/SIME-4Corners Images; © Frances Stephane/SIME-4Corners Images

The paper used for this book has been independently certified as having been sourced from well-managed forests and recycled wood or fibre according to the rules of the Forest Stewardship Council.
This book has been printed and bound in Italy by Printer Trento S.r.l., an FSC certified company for printing books on FSC mixed paper in compliance with the chain of custody and on products labelling standards.

FSC
Mixed Sources
Product group from well-managed forests and recycled wood or fibre
Cert no. CQ-COC-000012
www.fsc.org
© 1996 Forest Stewardship Council

Contents

Background 4–19
Introduction 4
The land 6
History 8
Politics 12
Culture 14
Festivals and events 18

Highlights 20–25
Highlights 20
Suggested itineraries 22

Destination guide 26–119
Beijing 26
The Forbidden City and Tiananmen Square 42
Beijing environs 52
Changcheng (Great Wall) 66
North of Beijing 72
South of Beijing 84
West of Beijing 106

Getting away from it all 120–25

Practical guide 126–57
When to go 126
Getting around 128
Accommodation 132
Food and drink 136
Entertainment 140
Shopping 144
Sport and leisure 146
Children 148
Essentials 150
Emergencies 156

Directory 158–73

Index 174–5

Maps
The land 7
Highlights 20
Beijing 27
Bike tour: Beijing 41
The Forbidden City and Tiananmen Square 43
Beijing environs 53
Changcheng (The Great Wall) 67
North of Beijing 73
South of Beijing 85
Song Shan scenic area 97
Walk: Qingdao 103
West of Beijing 107
Tour: Xian city 113

Features
Confucianism, Taoism and Buddhism 16
Chinese opera and circus 32
The imperial court 50
Chinese medicine 54
Development vs the environment 76
Rural life 88
Dayunhe (Grand Canal) 104
Marco Polo and the Silk Route 108
Inventions 114
The Long March 118

Walks, tours and drives
Bike tour: Beijing 40
Walk: Qingdao 102
Tour: Xian city 112

Introduction

China is far too vast and diverse a country to encapsulate in a few words, leaving both writers and visitors mumbling truisms such as 'fascinating' and 'mysterious'. Imperial China, Communist China, today's China, rural China, urban China, the China of your preconceptions, the China of slick government propaganda – the traveller will meet a dizzying blend of all these and more in anything other than a brief visit. Add to this mixture the current frenzied development and it can all seem a little overwhelming.

Nonetheless, travelling through China is bound to be an unforgettable experience. The country has the largest population on earth, a 5,000-year-old culture, a language spoken by one-fifth of humanity, and a deep desire to be counted among the ranks of the advanced nations. Despite this, China, particularly outside the big cities, makes few concessions (and often little sense) to foreign visitors.

Rewarding as China undoubtedly is, it is still a developing country. The pollution in cities and the poverty that still prevails in many rural areas contrast with breathtaking scenes of natural and man-made beauty. Many of China's best-known sights have been degraded by over-development. Fortunately, improved infrastructure and well-executed restorations have widened the number of historical sights that are accessible and well worth a visit.

Environmental degradation (*see pp76–7*) is also a serious issue for both the visitor and the Chinese people. Many Chinese cities are enshrouded in a permanent veil of air pollution, which is not only unattractive but a health concern, even for short-term visitors – nothing can dim an ardour for exploration like a nasty cough. Although the central government is taking steps to address this problem (for example, in 2007 Huang Shan, one of China's most beautiful mountains, was closed to visitors for a three-year period to allow the flora and fauna to recuperate), conservation and rapid development do not go hand in hand, and much remains to be done.

When, in the early 1980s, China allowed foreigners to visit for the first time since the 1949 Communist revolution, visitors were often shocked by the lack of connection that China and its people had with the rest of the world. Empty store shelves, a uniformly drab and impoverished population and few restaurants worthy of the name all sent visitors scurrying home. How times have changed. Beijing now has lodgings, restaurants and shopping to rival, if not exceed, the standards of Western cities.

Still, China remains a land of contrasts. Futuristic architecture and the latest fashions compete with the more traditional sights people come to see. China has the world's highest foreign exchange reserves and an economy bigger than Britain's, but peasants still plough their fields with water buffalo.

Possibly even more than most destinations, a visit to China requires an open frame of mind and a willingness to accept things as they are if you are to gain the insights that make the effort worthwhile. Travelling in China gives visitors a chance to try to unravel some of the strands in the ancient and modern Chinese puzzles, and to have some fun along the way.

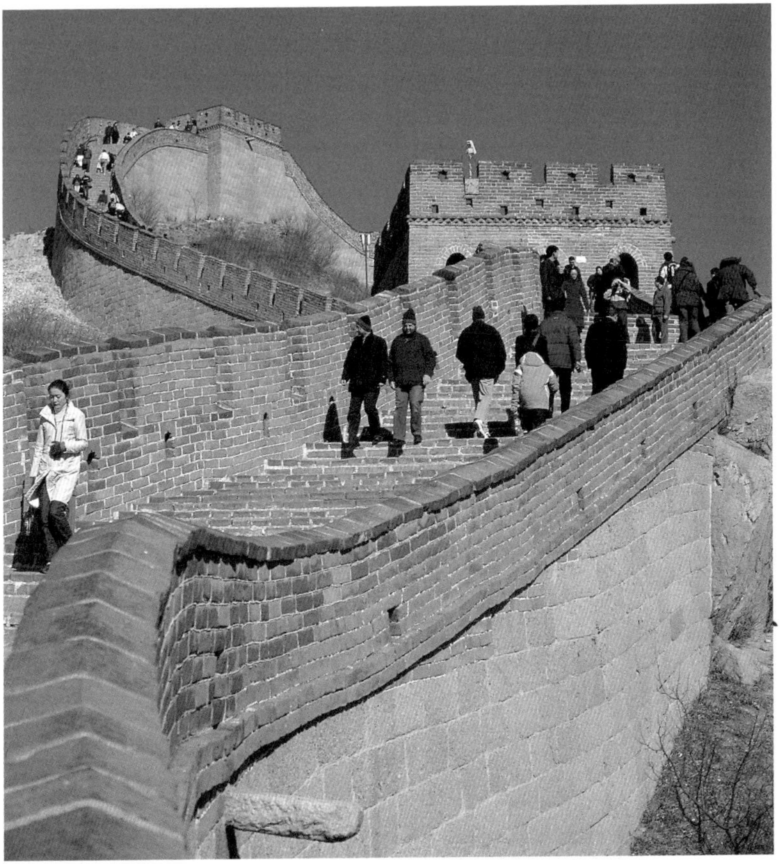

The Great Wall at Badaling

The land

China's North is the historical and cultural homeland of the Han Chinese people. China's main feature, the Yellow River, slices through this otherwise often arid region, and it gave rise to a population that long predates recorded history. Northern China's second defining feature is not natural but man-made. The famous Great Wall of China has come to symbolise many aspects of the country – an ancient and powerful civilisation, albeit insular and ultimately vulnerable.

Beijing, which means 'Northern Capital' in Chinese, lies on the country's northern periphery, and about 180km (110 miles) west of the Yellow Sea. The country's capital is fairly new in Chinese terms, but houses a wealth of cultural and historical sights.

China's landscapes can be majestic

Several capitals of ancient kingdoms flourished near the Yellow River, this life-giving (and taking, since it is prone to flooding) river, notably Xian, where Chinese civilisation is considered to have reached a cultural high point during the 8th century AD.

Outside the plains of the Yellow River, Northern China has a mountainous geography, and the interest of these peaks is enhanced by their religious significance. The Northeast region of China is part of what was once known as Manchuria, and is the ancestral homeland of China's last dynasty, the Qing.

Further afield, and even less 'Chinese' than the Northeast, lies the arid Northwest of China. The provinces of Qinghai and Gansu, as well as the autonomous regions of Ningxia and Xinjiang, all have fascinating relics remaining from the days of the Silk Road.

The autonomous region of Inner Mongolia lies along China's North Central border regions.

0 300km
0 150 miles
RUSSIAN FEDERATION
KAZAKHSTAN
MONGOLIA
CHINA
NORTH KOREA
SOUTH KOREA
NEPAL
Kyzyl
Irkutsk
Ulan-Ude
Chita
Tsagaannuur
Mörön
Darhan
Manzhouli
Bei'an
HEILONGJIAN
Hovd
Bulgan
ULAN BATOR
Ulan Bator-Buyant Ukha
Burqin
ALTAI MOUNTAINS
Qiqihar
Daqing
Harbin
Jixi
Karamay
Öndörhaan
Ulanhot
Altay
Arvayheer
Baruun Urt
Baicheng
Mudanjiang
Kuytun
Uliastai
Urumqi
Urumqi Diwopu International
Changchun
Qijiaojing
Saynshand
JILIN
Kanji
Aksu
Turpan
Dalandzadgad
Daban
Hami
Erenhot
Baishan
Changbai
Korla
INNER MONGOLIA
Chifeng
Shenyang
Dalain Hob
LIAONING
XINJIANG
Anxi
Hailaer
Jining
Beijing Shoudu Guoji Jichang
Jinzhou
Dunhuang
KOREA
Hohhot
Tangshan
PYONGYANG
Qiemo
Ruoqiang
Jiayuguan
Yellow River
Wuhai
BEIJING
Dalian
SEOUL
Jinchang
Tianjin
HEBEI
Great Wall of China
Wuzhong
Taiyuan
Yantai
Mangnai
Shijiazhuang
Yellow Sea
SHANXI
Xining
NINGXIA
Golmud
Jinan
Qingdao
Qinghai Lake
Lanzhou
SHANDONG
Plateau of Tibet
QINGHAI
Linxia
SHAANXI
Zhengzhou
Lianyungang
GANSU
Gêrzê
TIBET
Chindu
Tianshui
Xian
HENAN
JIANGSU
Amdo
Nanyang
Nanjing
Sogxian
Dêgê
Shanghai
SICHUAN
Suizhou
ANHUI
Shanghai-Pudong International
Zhabdün
Nagqu
Chamdo
Chengdu
Yangtze
HUBEI
Lhasa
Hangzhou
East China Sea
HIMALAYA MOUNTAINS
CHONGQING
Wuhan
Mount Everest
8848
Nyingchi
Rawu
Chongqing
ZHEJIANG
City
Large Town
Small Town
Main Road
Minor Road
Airport
International border
Regional border
Railway
N

History

Circa 2000 BC	Yangshao and Longshan cultures give rise to the Xia Dynasty, the first of the Chinese dynasties. Fine pottery produced.
1766–1122 BC	Shang Dynasty. Capital at Anyang, in present-day Henan Province. Jade and bronze decorative items are made.
1122–256 BC	Zhou Dynasty. Confucius formulates his code of ethics, Sun Tzu writes *The Art of War*, and the first Taoist texts are written.
221–206 BC	Qin Dynasty. Emperor Qin Shi Huang Di unites China. Chang'an (present-day Xian) is established as the capital. Weights, measures and currency are standardised. Construction of the Great Wall begins.
206 BC–AD 220	Han Dynasty. Trade routes developed along the Silk Road to Central Asia and the Middle East. Paper invented. Astronomers learn to predict eclipses. Buddhism arrives from India.
220–65	The Three Kingdoms. Internecine warfare between the states of Shu, Wei and Wu.
581–618	Sui Dynasty. Peace and unity are restored and a new capital is established at Luoyang. Work on the Grand Canal commences.
618–907	Tang Dynasty. A golden age for music, art and poetry, science and economic growth. The capital at Chang'an becomes one of the world's great cities. Chinese porcelain acquires a reputation for excellence.

Detail of bronze cowrie container from the Western Han Dynasty

Gunpowder invented. Woodblock printing begun and printing presses established. Empress Wu, China's first woman ruler, poisons her way to power and rules (690–705).

907–60 The Five Dynasties and Ten Kingdoms. A period of further internecine warfare.

907–1125 Liao Dynasty. Established by Khitan Tartars from Mongolia. Beijing's first turn at being a capital city, albeit one that controlled only Northern China.

960–1279 Song Dynasty. Capital at Kaifeng, in the Northern province of Henan, but later transferred to Hangzhou, dividing the dynasty into Northern and Southern Song periods. Opera developed, literature and landscape painting begin to flourish. Tea becomes popular throughout China.

1279–1368 Yuan Dynasty. The Mongols invade China and Kublai Khan sets up his capital at Dadu, present-day Beijing. Marco Polo visits China during this period.

1368–1644 Ming Dynasty. Han Chinese overthrow the Yuan and re-establish Chinese rule over a unified China. Zijin Cheng (the Forbidden City) is built at Beijing, the first time Beijing becomes the national capital of a truly Chinese dynasty. Maritime explorations to Indian Ocean and East Africa.

1644–1911 Qing Dynasty. Invading Manchus from the Northeast take advantage of an imperial court weakened by corruption to capture Beijing. Western colonial powers begin incursions into China.

1839–42 Chinese authorities seize Western opium at Canton, leading to the First Opium War the following year. China faces a century of imperialism.

1842 Treaty of Nanjing ends the war. Five treaty ports are opened to foreigners. Hong Kong is ceded to Britain.

1850–64 The anti-Manchu Taiping Rebellion devastates China.

1862 Dowager Empress Cixi is named regent and

	becomes de facto ruler of China.
1895	Treaty of Shimonoseki brings Sino-Japanese War (1894–5) to an end. Taiwan ceded to Japan.
1900	The Boxer Rebellion, an anti-foreign uprising, disrupts Beijing and encourages further foreign intervention.
1908	Emperor Pu Yi, China's last emperor, accedes to the throne.
1911	Emperor Pu Yi and the Qing Empire are overthrown by Sun Yatsen and like-minded nationalist revolutionaries. A period of instability follows.
1912	Republic of China is established on 1 January.
1921	Chinese Communist Party is formed in Shanghai.
1931	Japan invades Manchuria.
1934	Chinese Communists, led by Mao Zedong, begin their epic Long March.
1935	The Long March ends.
1937	War breaks out between China and Japan following the Marco Polo Bridge incident.
1945	Japan is defeated and Taiwan is returned to China.
1946	Civil war between Communists and Nationalist forces (Kuomintang) resumes.
1949	Communist forces control the mainland. Nationalist forces retreat to Taiwan. Mao Zedong declares founding of the People's Republic of China in Tiananmen Square on 1 October.
1957	Mao launches the Hundred Flowers Movement. By the end of the year more than 300,000 'rightists' are banished to the countryside or jailed.
1958	Mao launches the disastrous Great Leap Forward (a programme of rapid industrialisation), which leads to famine. Communes established.
1966	The Cultural Revolution begins as Mao issues a directive criticising senior

party officials. Bands of 'Red Guards' wreak havoc across the country.

1972 US President Richard Nixon visits Beijing, ending more than two decades of official enmity following the Korean War.

1976 Premier Zhou Enlai passes away in January. Mao dies in September.

1978 Deng Xiaoping assumes power and crushes ultra-leftist factions.

1989 The government kills hundreds of student demonstrators at Tiananmen Square in Beijing.

1990 Deng installs Jiang Zemin as his successor. The first stock exchange opens in Shanghai.

1997 Deng dies. Hong Kong is returned to the mainland.

1998 The Communist Party of China celebrates its first 50 years of rule. Portugal returns Macao to the Chinese.

2000 China joins the World Trade Organization.

2003 Businessmen are encouraged to join the Chinese Communist Party.

2004 Rights of private property are restored for the first time since 1949.

2008 China hosts the Olympics in Beijing.

THE CULTURAL REVOLUTION

Unleashed in 1966, this was Mao Zedong's attempt to free the Communist Party, society and culture from the 'old' values that were preventing the attainment of 'pure' Communism. For ten years, groups of 'Red Guards' composed of young workers and students were encouraged to attack all manifestations of authority except, of course, Mao himself. Temples were desecrated, schools and universities closed, teachers and factory managers tormented or worse, and millions sent to the countryside to 'learn from the peasants'. Finally the groups turned on each other, accusing their rivals of being 'imperialist spies' unworthy of the chairman. While Mao basked in the adulation of 1 million youths chanting his name in Tiananmen Square while holding his 'Red Book' of quotations aloft, cooler heads realised the country was descending into anarchy and called an end to the movement. Still, an inestimable price was paid in destroyed lives and property, including by the Guards themselves, who entered adulthood ignorant of all except chanted slogans. After Mao's death, the chaos was blamed on the 'Gang of Four', four top Communist Party officials, including Mao's wife, Jiang Qing, who later died in prison.

Politics

China's current political dynasty has clearly given priority to stability and material prosperity over democracy. Deng Xiaoping once remarked that the most basic of human rights is the right to eat. Still, it can be argued that only when the people feel that their interests are truly best represented by the government can true stability and prosperity flourish in China.

The People's Republic of China was proclaimed in 1949 after the Communist forces of Mao Zedong won a hard-fought war against the Nationalist Kuomintang government of Chiang Kai Shek. In the same year, Chiang fled to Taiwan (then known as Formosa). China became – or more accurately continued to be – a one-party state, this time with the Chinese Communist Party in the driving seat. Under the government's first five-year plan, great stress was placed on nationalisation, the development of heavy industry and the collectivisation of agriculture, the intention being to drag China from the feudal age into the modern world. The Great Leap Forward, initiated in 1958, emphasised the development of local political structures under Communist Party control, and the establishment of rural communes. It also led to the death of millions in the famine that followed.

Intellectuals had begun to chafe under the restrictions placed on their freedom of expression. In partial response to this, the party launched its Hundred Flowers Movement under the slogan: 'Let a Hundred Flowers Bloom and a Hundred Schools of Thought Contend'. Those who took advantage of the apparent openness to voice anti-government opinions were identified and purged. The struggle continued between those who supported Mao in preaching revolutionary fervour, and the pragmatists who were willing to ditch much Communist dogma in favour of progress – with the clear understanding that the party had absolutely no intention of relaxing its monopoly on political power.

As Mao and his supporters felt their control of the party slipping away to what they considered 'capitalist roaders', Mao struck back with the Great Proletarian Cultural Revolution in 1966. For ten years, China remained in the grip of an ailing Mao's obsession with permanent revolution. Youthful

'Red Guards' launched a wave of terror in which opponents were banished to the countryside, tortured or killed. Mao's death in 1976 and the arrest of his closest supporters (the so-called Gang of Four, including Mao's wife, Jiang Qing) cleared the way for Deng Xiaoping, who became the Communist Party Chairman in 1978.

Deng introduced more pragmatic policies in the economic sphere, famously announcing 'it is glorious to be rich', and flirting openly with capitalism, releasing the native energy and business skills of the Chinese, and allowing them to benefit personally while developing the country's overall economy.

Deng's legacy, however, was permanently scarred by the events of 3 and 4 June 1989, when his government ordered the suppression of pro-democracy demonstrations in Beijing, sparking the so-called 'Tiananmen Massacre'. Many innocent civilians and protesting students were mown down by the People's Liberation Army (PLA). Estimates of the dead range from 200 to 300 (Chinese government figures) to as high as 3,000 (Chinese student associations and Chinese Red Cross figures).

A policeman on duty

With the death of Deng in 1997, more freedom has been gradually given, although the Chinese Communist Party continues to hold ultimate power. Recent years have even seen a small-scale introduction of a voting system in some areas to elect village leaders and communities, pointing the way towards a kind of democracy. Indeed, former President Jiang Zemin and former premier Zhu Rongji did their utmost to promote international trade to make sure the open-door policy never slams shut – China's hosting of world summits such as APEC (Asia-Pacific Economic Cooperation) and of course the 2008 Olympics are major examples. China is today a member of the World Trade Organization; and Hong Kong and Macao's return to China have heralded a new tolerance of Western-style government. Despite many changes, political freedom lags far behind economic freedom. However, by and large, ordinary Chinese are focused on their new-found prosperity, while the Communist authorities concentrate on boosting international prestige and national pride through China's burgeoning space exploration programme and the 2008 Olympics, both of which are designed to show a more open and progressive face to the world.

Culture

It is fair to state that the people of Beijing and Northern China are more bound to traditional Chinese culture than those of the South. Not only is the region the cultural and historical wellspring of the Han culture, but generally speaking northerners like to consider themselves the 'true' followers of Chinese culture, less affected by foreign influences than their southern cousins.

In Beijing, the visitor has access to traditional architectural treasures, museums displaying fine examples of traditional paintings and ceramics, performances of Chinese opera, and a vibrant modern art scene.

Largely for linguistic reasons, it is the visual arts of China that are most appealing to non-Chinese. Chinese ceramics are a wonder to behold, from the delicate blue and white porcelains and deeply hued celadons to the unglazed Yixing teapots. Jade and other stone (as well as the currently disfavoured ivory) carvings are created with exquisite detail. China still produces fine silks, often intricately embroidered.

The Chinese, however, consider painting and calligraphy their highest visual art form. Traditional paintings are usually watercolours on scrolls of either paper or silk, which in some cases tell a story that develops as the scroll is unfurled. This is aided by the regular use of calligraphy in Chinese paintings – in fact some scrolls consist only of highly stylised Chinese characters.

Traditional Chinese music is typically instrumental, which makes it more accessible to foreigners. Classical Chinese music is both graceful and calming and an ideal accompaniment to a good cup of green tea. Typically, a small ensemble is composed of string, wind and percussion instruments.

FACE, AND HOW NOT TO LOSE IT

Face is important in China. It shows itself in subtle ways, particularly with foreign visitors. The more irritated a foreigner becomes at the lack of reaction of a Chinese (inscrutability, if you will) who doesn't seem to be getting the message, the smaller he becomes in the eye of the beholder. This can make travelling in China hard on the nerves, because the country throws up many situations that seem to call for vociferous complaint.

The Chinese are not averse to shouting among themselves, but foreigners should always be patient and understanding.

A venerable street musician

Chinese music of a much less calming genre finds its home in opera – between the lilting dialogues and clashing gongs it can be quite cacophonous, but great fun. Elaborate costumes, acrobatic clown roles and fantastic masks of make-up enliven the proceedings, especially for foreigners, who cannot be expected to follow the dialogue. Beijing is famous for its particular style of opera, called *jingju*.

Chinese traditional architecture is world-renowned for its distinctively elaborate yet graceful architectural forms, and Beijing abounds with fine examples of this heritage, despite the depredations of time, wars and now development. The complex symmetrical plans, colourful pavilions and curved roofs are not only attractive, but culturally relevant since many relate to traditional beliefs. For instance, the curved eaves function to launch malevolent forces back to the sky. *Feng shui*, or geomancy, which combines mystical formulas and design common sense, dictated classical architectural design and led to buildings of grace, style and practicality.

The modern art and cultural environment of China is not without interest. Chinese films, such as *Red Sorghum* and *Farewell My Concubine*, have received international acclaim – even while they are officially banned in China. Chinese painters and architects have established a reputation for innovation rather than mere derivative copies of Western motifs. While Beijingers certainly enjoy window-shopping in the glitzy Western-style malls of Wangfujing, they can also be found taking visible delight in the traditional architecture of the city's quiet parks and gardens.

An open-air game of draughts

Confucianism, Taoism and Buddhism

Confucianism

The stereotypical 'Chinaman' of Hollywood films was always ready with some anodyne saying from Confucius, reflecting the fact that Confucian thought still permeates Chinese society, as it has done for 2,500 years. Many educated Chinese can quote knowledgeably from the great philosopher, whose real name was Kong Fuzi, meaning the Master Kong.

Statue of Confucius

Born in the 6th century BC at Qufu in the state of Lu (present-day Shandong Province), Confucius spent most of his life as a government official. The Confucian Analects, compiled after his death, are a collection of his sayings and actions, which are themselves based on ancient Chinese teachings and precepts. Confucius believed the origins of nature are to be found in the yin-yang, passive-active principles, which form a harmony when combined. In practice, he stressed social justice, filial piety and the obligations of the ruler towards the ruled and vice versa. The religious element in his teaching was based on the notion that if individuals and society behaved properly, heaven would leave them in peace.

Taoism

Taoism is based on the teachings of Lao Zi, meaning the Old Master, a 6th-century BC philosopher. Nothing is known about the life of Lao Zi (who may actually be legendary). His teachings, compiled in the 3rd century BC, were at least partly in competition with those of Confucius. In the collection of sacred Taoist texts called

Dao De Jing, the Tao, or Way, is the hidden principle at the heart of the universe, a principle which can be touched by those prepared to live in harmony with nature and the environment. This was in contrast to the focus on right behaviour and good deeds advocated by Confucius. As Taoism developed, its belief system also incorporated the yin–yang (female–male) system of balancing opposites.

Buddhism

Buddhism arrived in China from India. Karma is Buddhism's main doctrine: the belief that good and evil deeds beget their own reward, both in this life and more so in the future through reincarnation. By the time of its widespread acceptance in China, Buddhism had undergone significant changes. The concept of Paradise became a key part of Chinese Buddhism in the Mahayana form called Chan in China, a variation of which took root in Japan as Zen. The idea that a Buddhist monk should be able to look after himself led to the foundation of the Shaolin Monastery near Dengfeng, in Henan Province, where the kung fu form of self-defence combat was developed.

Modern beliefs

Today, the officially atheist government has softened its stance on religious practice and many sacred sites of all faiths have even been restored. The Han Chinese are not (nor ever were) adherents of a single faith, but choose elements of each religion that appeal to them to form a syncretic belief system. Muslim Chinese are an exception to this. Christianity is also gaining popularity, especially among the young. Older people continue to go on pilgrimages to temples or holy mountains, and the younger generation now make tentative and awkward, but visibly heartfelt, offerings at religious sites.

Incense is offered along with prayers at all temples

Festivals and events

Festivals form an important part of China's respect for the past, although not all are public holidays. This is a selection of the more important festivals celebrated either nationally or specifically in Beijing and Northern China. Note that traditional Chinese festivals are based on the Lunar Calendar so the specific dates vary from year to year. If you are in China around the approximate dates, ask around for specifics.

January/February

Beijing Longqing Gorge Ice and Snow Festival If Heilongjiang isn't on your itinerary, this display of ice sculptures is held 80km (50 miles) outside of Beijing in January.

Harbin Ice Lantern Festival The people of Heilongjiang Province create fabulous, lit-up ice sculptures. 5 January–5 February.

Spring Festival Also known as Chinese New Year. Mainly celebrated at home, but public parks fill up with families in their new finery, houses are decorated and firecrackers chase away the evil spirits. Late January or early February.

February/March

Lantern Festival Home-made lanterns are displayed on the 15th day of the first lunar month, a full moon marking the end of New Year celebrations. Mid-February–mid-March.

April

Qing Ming Honouring ancestors by cleaning their tombs and placing flowers on them, usually followed by a picnic at the tomb. Early April.

Luoyang Peony Fair The peony is celebrated against the backdrop of Luoyang's giant Buddha rock sculptures. More than a million blooms are on display in city parks. 15–25 April.

Weifang International Kite Festival Home of the International Kite Federation and a Kite Museum, Weifang (in Shandong Province) displays its love affair with kites. 20–25 April.

May

International Labour Day A week-long holiday for all Chinese, so travel can be difficult, but Beijing hosts an impressive parade and people-watching is great throughout the country. 1 May.

June

Dragon Boat Festival Held on the full moon of the fifth lunar month in June, decorated traditional boats are raced in honour of Qu Yuan, a poet who drowned himself in the 3rd century BC to protest against imperial corruption. In Beijing, races are held on the lakes.

August

Nadam Fair and Grassland Tourism Festival Held at Hohhot, capital of Inner Mongolia, this features folklore and traditional products, and also a flower fair and tour of Wudang Lamasery. 15–25 August.

Xinjiang Grape Festival The Yuelu Caravan of Camels is the highlight of this festival in Turpan that recalls life along the ancient Silk Route. 20–26 August.

September/October

Xian Ancient Culture and Art Festival Pageants recall the ancient cultures of this former capital of China, close to the site of the terracotta warriors. 9–15 September.

Shaolin Martial Arts Festival The monks of Mount Song Shan (Henan Province) display their martial arts skills. 10–15 September.

Birthday of Confucius This celebrates the great Chinese sage throughout China, especially in his home town of Qufu in Shandong Province. Late September–early October.

Mid-Autumn Festival Essentially a harvest festival celebrated throughout the country on the full moon of the eighth lunar month. Temples are lighted in the evening, and locals have barbecues in the parks, eating moon cakes while admiring the moon. Late September–early October.

National Day On 1 October in 1949, Mao Zedong declared the founding of the People's Republic of China in Tiananmen Square. It is now the occasion for a massive (largely military) parade along Chang'an Jie, as well as a week-long holiday for all Chinese, making travel and accommodation a challenge. 1 October.

General

Kaizhai Festival This Islamic festival celebrates the end of the fasting month of Ramadan. Since Islam uses a strictly lunar calendar, the three-day festival can fall any time during the Gregorian calendar. Near any mosque you will find music, sweetmeats and general merry-making.

Kites are Chinese innovations

Highlights

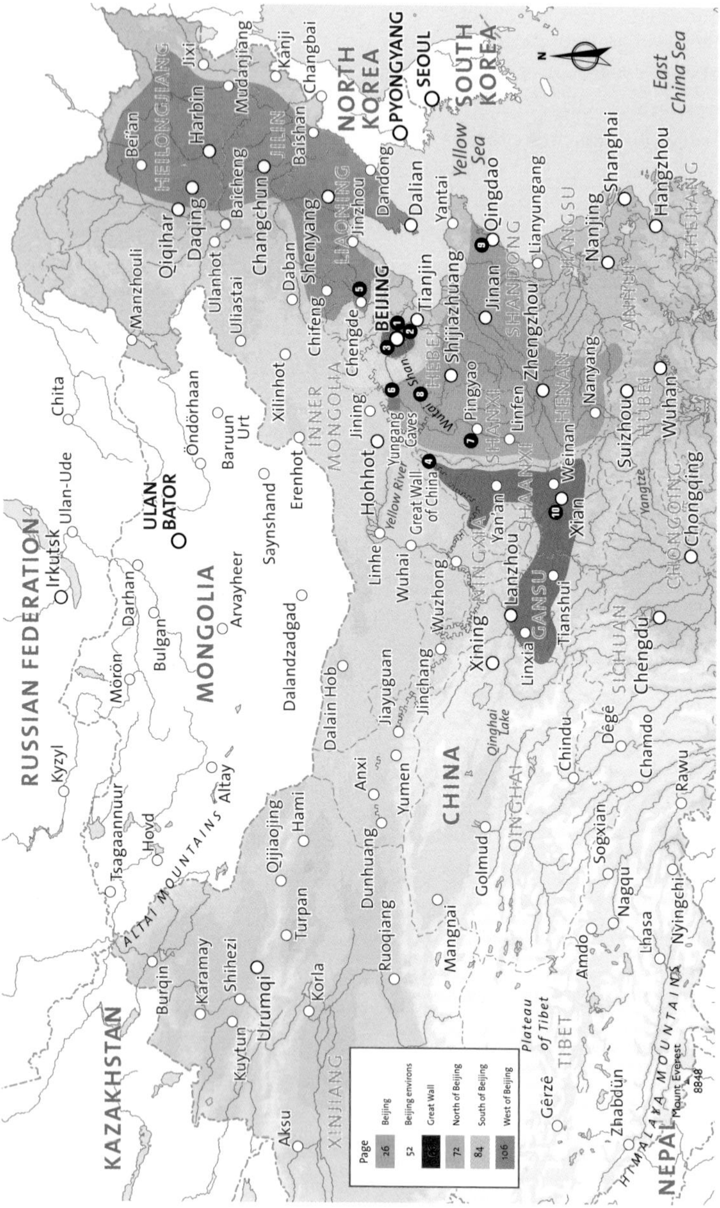

RUSSIAN FEDERATION
MONGOLIA
CHINA
KAZAKHSTAN
NORTH KOREA
SOUTH KOREA
NEPAL
BEIJING
ULAN BATOR
PYONGYANG
SEOUL
Yellow Sea
East China Sea
Plateau of Tibet
ALTAI MOUNTAINS
HIMALAYA MOUNTAINS
Mount Everest
8848
Great Wall of China
Yungang Caves
Wutai Shan
Yellow River
Yangtze
Qinghai Lake
HEILONGJIANG
JILIN
LIAONING
INNER MONGOLIA
HEBEI
SHANXI
SHANDONG
HENAN
SHAANXI
NINGXIA
GANSU
QINGHAI
XINJIANG
TIBET
SICHUAN
CHONGQING
HUBEI
ANHUI
JIANGSU
ZHEJIANG
Harbin
Changchun
Shenyang
Dalian
Tianjin
Shijiazhuang
Jinan
Qingdao
Zhengzhou
Pingyao
Datong
Hohhot
Xian
Lanzhou
Xining
Chengdu
Chongqing
Wuhan
Nanjing
Shanghai
Hangzhou
Urumqi
Lhasa
Page
26 Beijing
52 Beijing environs
Great Wall
72 North of Beijing
84 South of Beijing
106 West of Beijing

1. **Forbidden City** Located in the heart of Beijing, this huge walled compound was the imperial palace of China's last two dynasties, the Ming and the Qing (*see p42*).

2. **Temple of Heaven** Just south of the Forbidden City, this is where the emperor performed the sacred rites confirming his role as the Son of Heaven. The temple features magnificent ceremonial halls (*see pp29–31*).

3. **Summer Palace** Just north of Beijing, this is where the later Qing rulers (notably, the Dowager Empress Cixi) relaxed in idyllic splendour while their empire collapsed around them (*see pp62–5*).

4. **Great Wall of China** There are several places north of Beijing where you can see and walk on top of this iconic structure that at one time stretched along the entire northern Chinese frontier (*see pp66–71*).

5. **Imperial Palace at Chengde** Surrounded by mountains in Shanxi Province, northeast of Beijing, the early Qing emperors came here to get away from the wiles of the capital and back to their Manchu roots. Outside the royal compound they built Lamaist temples to welcome their guests from Tibet (*see pp74–5 & pp78–9*).

6. **Yungang Caves** Magnificent early Buddhist statuary and temples built inside caves dug in cliff faces during the 5th century AD (*see pp85–6*).

7. **Pingyao** During the Qing Dynasty this was the banking capital of China; now this small town in Shanxi Province is a living museum of life in China during the 19th century (*see pp86–7*).

8. **Wutai Shan** The village of Taihuai is surrounded by dozens of temples in the surrounding hills (*see pp90–91*).

9. **Qingdao** Located on the Yellow Sea in Shandong Province, this charming city was colonised by the Germans, who left behind an amazing architectural legacy (*see pp100–101*).

10. **Terracotta Army** Built 2,000 years ago on the orders of Qin Shi Huang, the emperor who united China into a single country, these life-size sculptures, designed to protect the emperor in the afterlife, were only uncovered by a well digger in 1974 (*see pp116–117*).

Suggested itineraries

These itineraries will let you see as much of the destination as time allows. They are admittedly fast paced, and you will of course have special interests and choose to focus more on some areas or on types of sights than on others.

Long weekends

Have dinner at one of the charming lakeside restaurants along Qianhai Lake followed by a stroll. You'll find good places for a quiet nightcap here, but if you're in the mood for something livelier, take a cab to the Chaoyang District and follow your ears to music that suits you.

Missing the Great Wall of China is just not permitted. If you go to the closest area at Badaling, you can also see the nearby Ming Tombs, but if you opt for the more distant sites, such as Mutianyu and Simatai, you can enjoy the countryside en route and avoid the crowds. Make an early evening of it at the night market at Wangfujing, which by day is Beijing's posh shopping district, but in the evening has plenty of light food and souvenir shopping.

Go to Zijin Cheng (the Forbidden City), Beijing's magnificent imperial palace, then walk across the Socialist Realism of Tiananmen Square, visiting Chairman Mao's Mausoleum if you are so inclined. At Qianmen Gate, either walk or take a taxi to the Temple of Heaven. Then take a taxi to the nearby

Scenes from Chinese history in the Long Corridor of the Summer Palace

Pavilions on the lake at the Imperial Summer Resort, Chengde

Dazhalan, a neighbourhood of restored *hutongs* (Beijing's traditional lanes) now given over to shopping. Alternatively, if you're a determined shopper, take a taxi to Pajiayuan, Beijing's huge weekend market, which is at its best on Sunday morning.

One-week trips

Start with Beijing, as shown for the long weekend above, then visit the Summer Palace, where China's last emperors and empresses enjoyed the final years of their epoch, and return to the city in the afternoon to take in the Ming Dynasty pavilions on Coal Hill, which is located directly behind the Forbidden City and affords good views over central Beijing. Afterwards, enjoy the willow trees and vaulted bridges in nearby Beihai Park.

Make the 250km (155-mile) journey to the imperial resort at Chengde on a modern expressway. Here the Qing emperors enjoyed manly pursuits such as horse riding and archery, and met diplomats from as far away as Burma, Tibet, Xinjiang and England. In 1793, the British envoy Lord Macartney met Emperor Qianlong here to seek trade with China and came away empty-handed. Explore the palace and cycle to the outlying temples that have Lamaist architectural motifs, including one built to resemble the Potala Palace in Lhasa.

Xian is your next stop with its restored city wall, the Drum and Bell Towers, an excellent history museum, the Great Mosque and the very famous Terracotta Army sights. The Taoist Eight Immortals temple is nearby.

The Terracotta Army, comprising of over 7,000 life-size figurines, including archers and cavalry with their steeds, has been uncovered in three major excavation pits. All different and formed in exquisite detail, they were created over 2,000 years ago to guard the nearby tomb of the megalomaniacal emperor Qin Shi Huang, which has not yet been excavated. There is a good exhibition hall at the site with informative displays.

Return to Beijing. The Fragrant Hills make a good day outing for your final day.

Two-week trips

To the previous itinerary, add a trip to Datong, which can be reached by car in about four hours from Beijing, and explore the old city. Don't miss the ancient Huayan Temple from the Liao Dynasty and the Nine Dragons Screen, an intricately tiled spirit wall from the Ming Dynasty. Visit the magnificent Yungang caves, located a short drive outside Datong. These powerful examples of Buddhist art were carved into sandstone cliffs during the 5th century AD. The statues show significant influences of Indian, Persian and even Greek artistic traditions.

The drive to Taihuai, south of Datong, takes about four hours. This small town owes its existence to the surrounding temples of Wutai Shan. Some of these mountaintop temples are accessible by cable car, and the forests surrounding the temples are good for a peaceful stroll with well-marked trails.

Terracotta warriors at Xian

WHAT'S A *HUTONG*?

Visitors to Beijing will likely hear of '*Hutong* Tours' and will understandably wonder what they will see if they go. The word *hutong* refers to the narrow alleyways of Bejing lined with courtyard houses called *siheyuan*. The structures first appeared during the Mongolian Yuan Dynasty and the word is of Mongolian origin, coming from either the word *huotuan*, meaning 'passageway', or *huttog*, meaning 'water well'.

Hutongs covered most of Bejing as late as the early 20th century, but were one of the first targets of the wreckers' ball when the city began to modernise. Fortunately, many still remain and are lively neighbourhoods that offer a glimpse of the everyday life of Beijingers. Tourists can either walk or be pedalled through the *hutong* – it is a pleasant escape from the steel and glass of today's Beijing.

You can then fly to Xian from Taiyuan and visit the Longmen Caves, just outside Luoyang. After the Northern Wei Dynasty moved its capital from Datong to Luoyang, these creators of the Yungang Caves continued their work here. The later Sui and Tang dynasties' emperors carried on the work, and the artistic evolution is interesting to observe. Another flight will take you to Qingdao to visit the old city and beaches. The old city is an amazing example of European architecture in Asia. It was German territory for only about 50 years, and they built many structures of Bavarian and Teutonic origin, including the first brewery (the famous Tsingtao brand). The former governor's palace, two churches and many opulent villas are all located within a short distance of each other, and the old brewery is a fun museum.

Longer visits

Depending on the time of year, and your own tolerance for climatic extremes, either add the Northeast cities of Shenyang and Harbin, or alternatively continue east from Xian to the Silk Road sights in Gansu and Xinjiang. A trip along the Silk Road ought to include Gansu's Dunhuang with its fabulous Buddhist Mogao Caves. Once into Xinjiang, the legendary oasis town of Turpan and its satellite ancient cities provide further diversions. Kashgar, in the far west, is the best place from which to organise trips into the Pamir Mountains and beyond into Central Asia.

The tomb of Emperor Qin Shi Huang in Xian

Beijing

Beijing, which in Chinese means 'Northern Capital', is a city of 14 million residents and, of course, the capital of the nation. Beijing was also the capital of the last two Chinese dynasties, the Ming and the Qing, and many of their palaces, ceremonial sites and temples remain and have been restored to their earlier splendour.

Political power and recent history all radiate from here – from the profoundly imperial ambience of Zijin Cheng (the Forbidden City) to the vastness of Tiananmen Square, Beijing exudes power. While Shanghai and Guangzhou, among other cities, are far more vibrant commercially, Beijing is the city of grace and style, with wide avenues, spacious parks, and a wealth of important historical and cultural sites worth visiting.

At the centre of the city lies the huge complex of royal residences and audience halls known as the Forbidden City. The rest of Beijing seems to emerge from this centre in concentric lines, with the historic area of Qianmen and the Temple of Heaven to the south; the modern shopping area of Wangfujing, the Tibetan Buddhist Lama Temple and the Chaoyang entertainment district to the east; and the pleasant lake district and the university quarter to the west.

Beijing is a study in change and contrasts. The famous *hutongs*, or alleys, and the old courtyard houses (*siheyuan* in Chinese) that line these ancient lanes are disappearing as high-rise buildings take their place. Still, old Beijing survives and many restorations

Beihai Park was once the private retreat of emperors

of once dilapidated ancient sites have made them more accessible and interesting to visitors.

SOUTHERN BEIJING

Baiyunguan (Temple of the White Cloud)

Taoism is represented in this part of Beijing to the northeast of the mosque, where elaborately dressed Taoist priests perform ceremonies of this most uniquely Chinese of faiths. Elaborate iconography and a series of maze-like courtyards merit a visit. If you're in Beijing during Chinese New Year, don't miss the temple fair here.

6 Baiyunguan Jie. Tel: (010) 6340 4812. Open: 8.30am–4.30pm. Admission charge. Metro: Nanlishilu.

Fayuan Si (Temple of the Source of Buddhist Teaching)

Founded in AD 696, this is the oldest Buddhist temple in Beijing. A vast and

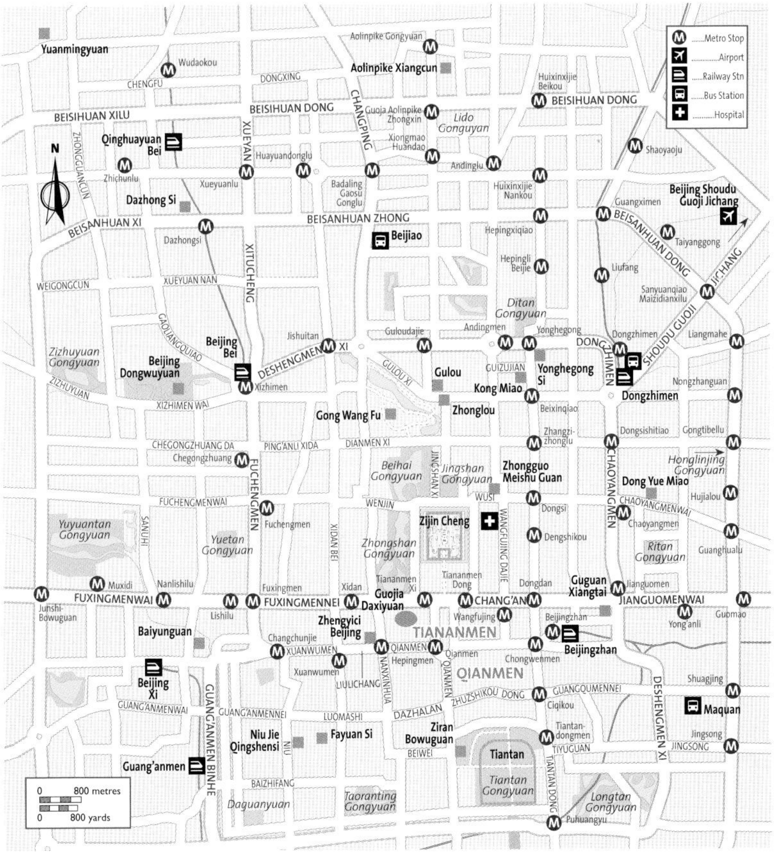

attractive complex, it contains an academy for training monks, a library, and several halls with a variety of Buddhist statuary from the laughing Maitreya Buddha statues to more austere incarnations such as the sedate reclining Buddha. In addition to the excellent exhibitions of Buddhist art, the architecture and atmosphere are quite relaxing.

7 Fayuan Qianjie. Tel: (010) 6353 4171. Open: 8am–3pm. Admission charge. Metro: Xuanwumen.

Niu Jie Qingshensi (Cow Street Mosque)

The oldest and largest mosque in Beijing is just west of Fayuan Si, the Buddhist temple, but a cultural world apart. The mosque itself, like many in China, looks more Chinese than Middle Eastern with its curved eaves and tiled roof, but the interior is adorned with verses from the Koran and the geometric designs that characterise Islamic art. There are over 6 million Muslims in China. Some are not ethnically Chinese, but others, called the Hui, are distinguished from the Han majority only by their faith and dietary traditions. A mosque has existed on this site since AD 966, although the structure has been rebuilt many times. The courtyard is lush and relaxing, and the main prayer hall ornate. Conservative dress makes you feel more welcome. Surrounding the mosque is a Muslim neighbourhood with little

Cow Street Mosque

restaurants and street vendors selling kebabs and flatbreads.
88 Niu Jie. Tel: (010) 6353 2564. Open: 9am–9pm. Closed: to visitors on Friday, the Muslim Sabbath. Admission charge. Metro: Xuanwumen.

Qianmen District

Directly south of Tiananmen Square, you will find this lively area. During the Qing Dynasty, Chinese citizens were allowed to live only in this area, with the more salubrious areas around the lakes reserved for the ruling Manchus. During that time the area acquired the reputation as the entertainment district, filled with theatres, restaurants, wine shops, and more than a few houses of ill-repute. Today it is noted for its interesting shops, walking streets and traditional architecture. Dazhalan and Liulichang, two traditional shopping areas of Beijing, have been restored and are vehicle-free zones. They are great places for browsing the shops that sell arts and crafts, used books (both Chinese and English), scroll paintings, paper lanterns and much more. The oldest traditional Chinese medicine shop in the country and the famous teashops selling the best of Chinese teas are found in Qianmen, as is the **Zhengyici Beijing Opera Theatre**, a beautifully restored 18th-century wooden building with regular performances in the evening.
All these sights are within walking distance of the Hepingmen Metro, and are open until late evening.

Temple of Heaven – the Hall of Prayer for Good Harvests

Tiantan (Temple of Heaven)

Located in the southeast of Beijing, this is one of the city's most impressive sights. Each emperor of the Ming and Qing dynasties used this magnificent temple complex to fulfil the most important rites that confirmed his position as the Son of Heaven – in effect an arbiter between humans and the gods. Ancestor worship lay at the heart of these rites, which sometimes lasted for several days, especially at the harvest time and the winter solstice. Since bad harvests or other natural disasters were considered to be caused by the emperor's loss of the Mandate of

Heaven, and a legitimate reason for his replacement, all in power, and those who wished to seize it, took these rites quite seriously. The temple complex is now a public park and very popular among locals seeking respite from the city's noise, but it still retains the powerful and dignified atmosphere of a once sacred centre of worship.

Like most imperial monuments, it is built on a vast scale, covering 272ha (672 acres). The most impressive structure, in the centre of the complex, is the 38m (125ft) high **Qiniandian (Hall of Prayer for Good Harvests)** built on a three-level marble terrace with walls of vividly painted wood and a blue-tiled roof – blue being the symbolic colour of heaven. Inside, 28 massive columns of red and gold painted pine, imported from the Southwest province of Yunnan, support the roof. The hall was originally built in AD 1420, during the Ming Dynasty, and rebuilt in 1889 after it was destroyed by fire – the fire seen doubtlessly as an inauspicious event during the fading days of the Qing rulers.

South of this formidable structure lies the **Huangqiongyu (Imperial Vault of Heaven)**, where the emperor donned his ceremonial robes appropriate to the rite he would perform. Within this hall lie stone ancestral tablets believed to hold the spirits of the royal ancestors. Surrounding the hall, the **Huiyin Bi (Echo Wall)** will carry voices great distances – as long as there aren't too many people attempting this feat simultaneously. Just south of the **Hall of Heaven**, the **Yuanqiu (Altar of Heaven)**

Imperial Vault of Heaven

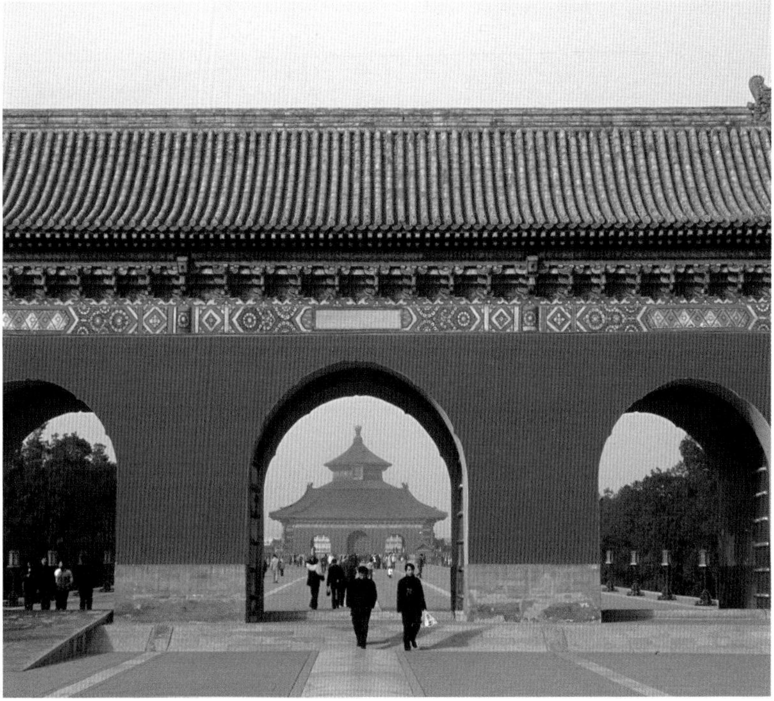

Entrance to the Temple of Heaven Park

is where the emperor made sacrifices to the gods during the winter solstice. A three-level stone terrace surrounded by two walls, the stone slab in the centre of this altar was considered the very centre of the world in Imperial China. In the west of the park lies the **Zhaigong (Hall of Abstinence)**, where the emperor would fast prior to the rites. If you leave the complex by the west gate, you'll cross the **Tianqiao (Heavenly Bridge)** and enter a traditional residential area of the city. If you leave via the east, over the **Hongqiao (Red Bridge)**, you'll come across the Hong Qiao Market, which sells antiques and pearls.

Tiantan Dong. Tel: (010) 6702 2617.
Open: 8am–5.30pm.
Admission charge. Metro: Qianmen.

Ziran Bowuguan (Museum of Natural History)

This museum, adjacent to Tiantan (Temple of Heaven), contains an impressive collection of flora and fauna, including a complete dinosaur skeleton and a section on human evolution.

126 Tianqiao Nan.
Tel: (010) 6702 4431.
Open: 8.30am–5pm. Admission charge.
Metro: Qianmen.

Chinese opera and circus

Chinese opera

Chinese drama, including what is known abroad as Beijing opera, began rather late in China's cultural evolution, during the Yuan Dynasty (1279–1368), although it drew on older storytelling traditions. Beijing opera (which is only one of 300 different forms of traditional opera) only really flowered during the Qing Dynasty, from the 18th century. It is characterised by exaggerated and stylised actions (generally performed by men), and high-pitched singing accompanied by a piercing string and percussion ensemble. It is not to everyone's taste, although it is interesting to see at least once. The themes are usually romantic in the broad sense, with characters using their skill to overcome natural disasters, rebellion or some other calamity. The high-pitched singing and music styles developed out of the

Chinese opera is a highly stylised art

Chinese circus performers' skills are world-famous

need to project over chattering crowds in such noisy performance venues as markets and teahouses. Authentic Chinese opera is still a form of street theatre, but you can also see it in the more formal context of the theatre. Visually, the costumes are the most striking feature, and the style of the clothes and of the make-up gives clues to the characters' true natures.

Circus

Chinese circus does not involve animals and is all about acrobatics, performed by troupes and individuals whose skills are legendary. Plate-spinning and performing handstands on a pagoda of chairs are the least of the marvels. The skills originated with popular street theatre and are emblematic of religious festivals, sacrificial rites, and themes from daily life, although they have since moved to the more sophisticated venue of the gymnasium. Acrobatics have a long history in China, but the first state acrobatic troupe was not formed until 1950 in Beijing.

EASTERN BEIJING

Dong Yue Miao (Eastern Peak Temple)

Located near the Workers' Stadium in the Chaoyang District (better known for its restaurants and nightlife), this striking and beautiful Taoist temple commemorates the spirit of Tai Shan (also known as Dong Yue, meaning 'eastern summit'), the mountain in Shandong Province that is holy to the faith. The temple is quite active, with Taoist priests performing ceremonies in honour of the myriad deities they revere. The collection of statuary is amazing, with both gods and demons portrayed. The role and significance of each of these vivid and sometimes outrageous looking characters is explained in English captions.

141 Chaoyangmenwai. Tel: (010) 6551 0151. Open: 8am–4pm. Admission charge. Metro: Chaoyangmen.

Guguan Xiangtai (Ancient Observatory)

The tower was built in 1437 to house the astronomical observatory. During the Qing Dynasty, the Jesuits taught modern astronomical techniques to the Chinese, who used them largely for astrological calculations. Now a museum displays an interesting collection of astronomical devices, some locally constructed, others gifts to the emperor such as an azimuth from Louis XIV.

2 Dongbiao Bei Hutong, off Jianguomenwai. Tel: (010) 6524 2202/ 2246. Open: Wed–Sun 9–11am, 1–4pm.

The Ancient Observatory

Closed: Mon & Tue. Admission charge. Metro: Jianguomen.

Kong Miao (Confucius Temple)

This temple was founded in 1302, but, unlike many other cultural treasures of Beijing, it has not been restored to its original function and now operates as the Capital Museum, displaying artefacts relevant to the city's history. Confucian philosophy, with its emphasis on hierarchy, was perceived as particularly 'feudal' as opposed to the 'egalitarian' ideology of Communism.

Those expecting the vibrant atmosphere of a Buddhist temple will find the place rather austere. Confucian philosophy stressed order and correct behaviour in this life, not the seeking of divine intercession through supplication to ancient gods. Its main interest lies in its inscribed stone tablets that give the name and home towns of those successfully passing the imperial examinations, which essentially consisted of memorising the Confucian classic texts.

13 Guizujian. Tel: (010) 8401 1977. Open: 9am–4pm. Admission charge. Metro: Yonghegong.

Wangfujing (Wangfujing Street)

The shopping street is within walking distance of the Forbidden City and serves as a cultural counterpoint for those who revel in contrasts. This street is China's temple to modernity and consumerism, with Cartier and Versace the gods. There are several shopping malls and department stores, and it is certainly worth a stroll, mainly for people-watching. There are some interesting boutiques showing the works of local designers, as well as souvenir items for tourists, but most of the imported goods on display here are considerably more expensive than you would find at home. It becomes more interesting in the evening when food sellers set up mobile restaurants on the street.

Shops open: 10am–10pm. Metro: Wangfujing.

Monsters line up on the Lama Temple roof to ward off evil spirits

Yonghegong Si (Lama Temple)

An extraordinarily large temple, Yonghegong owes its imposing lines

Ice covers the lake in Beihai Park in winter

partly to its remodelling in 1694 to serve as the residence of the future emperor, Yongzheng. Today, it is an important repository of Tibetan and Mongolian Buddhist images and works of art. The series of enclosures and pavilions includes a 26m (85ft) statue of the Maitreya Buddha carved from a single piece of sandalwood, the biggest of many Buddha images inside.
12 Yonghegong. Tel: (010) 6404 3769. Open: 9am–4.30pm. Admission charge. Metro: Yonghegong.

Zhongguo Meishu Guan (National Art Museum of China)

Formerly the Peking University building, opened to the public in 1959 and recently totally refurbished, this gallery features constantly changing exhibitions of Chinese arts, both traditional and modern. Check the entertainment magazines for current exhibitions.
1 Wusi. Tel: (010) 6401 6234. Open: Tue–Sun 9am–5pm. Closed: Mon. Admission charge. Metro: Dongsi.

THE LAKE DISTRICT AND WESTERN BEIJING

Beihai Gongyuan (Beihai Park)

There can be few more beautiful city parks in the world than this graceful former retreat of the emperors, situated slightly north and west of the Forbidden City. It is a perfect place to escape the bustle of the city and watch

Beijingers doing the same. Located on the site of a 10th-century palace, many of its structures are reconstructions of originals dating from the 15th to the 17th centuries. Covering almost 70ha (173 acres), half of the park is taken up by Beihai Lake, which hosts ice skaters when frozen in the winter and pedal-powered boats during the other seasons. The park is notable for the Round City, an area established by the Mongol Emperor Kublai Khan (1214–94) for his palace. At the heart of Beihai Lake is the Qiong Island, a man-made hill that affords panoramic views over the Forbidden City. At the summit of the hill you will find the ghostly bubble of the White Dagoba Buddhist stupa built under the direction of the then Dalai Lama when he visited Beijing in 1651.
1 Wenjin. Tel: (010) 6403 2244. Open: 7am–7pm. Admission charge. Metro: Tiananmen Xi.

Beijing Dongwuyuan (Beijing Zoo)

Over recent years the Beijing Zoological authorities have made great strides to improve the general standard of the zoo. The world-famous pandas have a much improved house and the new aquarium with its shark hall is touted as the world's biggest inland aquarium.
137 Xizhimen Wai. Tel: (010) 6831 4411. Zoo open: 7.30am–5.30pm; Panda Hall open: 8am–5pm. Admission charge. Metro: Xizhimen.

Dazhong Si (Great Bell Temple)

The Great Bell Temple is appropriately named, since it houses the biggest bell in China, weighing almost 47 tonnes (46 tons), and is covered in Buddhist scriptures. During the Ming and Qing dynasties, the bell was rung only to record the arrival of the new year. It was cast between 1403 and 1424, and a special canal had to be dug to move it to its final home after it had been cast. When winter came, the bell was loaded on to a sledge and dragged over the frozen canal surface. This spacious compound also houses a collection of

White Pagoda in Beihai Park

traditional bells even older than the main attraction.
31A Beisanhuan Xi. Tel: (010) 6255 0843. Open: 8.30am–4.30pm. Admission charge. Metro: Dazhongsi.

Gong Wang Fu (Palace of Prince Gong)

North of Beihai Park, this beautifully restored mansion was once the home of a Ming Dynasty prince, a brother of the emperor who ruled as regent for two Ming-era boy emperors. The compound features elaborate gardens with pleasure pavilions and fish pools. The main structure is equally ornate and contains a theatre where traditional Chinese music is performed by students of the Chinese Conservatory of Music, which is located within the palace grounds. The *hutongs* surrounding the palace also merit a visit.
17 Qianhai Xi. Tel: (010) 6616 8149. Open: 8.30am–5pm. Admission charge. Metro: Guloudajie.

Contemplation on Coal Hill

OTHER PARKS

In addition to the parks described here, other valuable patches of green include Ditan Park, Longtan Park and Taoranting Park. Ditan, to the north of the Lama Temple, offers pleasantly shaded walks and a small museum. Longtan, to the east of the Temple of Heaven Park, is the place to go for roller coasters and other fun-fair rides. Finally, Taoranting, to the west of the Temple of Heaven Park, is one of Beijing's oldest parks and is a popular place to swim.

Jingshan Gongyuan (Coal Hill)

This five-peaked artificial hill provided the Ming emperors with a view over the city from within their private park, the site and design of which were chosen according to the principles of *feng shui* (Chinese geomancy). Something may have been wrong in the calculations, since the last Ming emperor committed suicide here while fleeing a peasant uprising. Now open to the public, the park still has superb views, and splendid pavilions from which to appreciate them.
44 Jingshan Xi. Located just to the north of the Forbidden City.
Tel: (010) 6404 4071. Open: 6am–9pm. Admission charge. Metro: Dongsi.

Old Summer Palace

Yuanmingyuan (Old Summer Palace)

In 1860, European troops destroyed the buildings of the Old Summer Palace, originally laid out in the 12th century. Ironically, this gave Beijing one of its most beautiful sights, for at times when the Summer Palace is mobbed, the gardens remain a sea of tranquillity. Some trees have been planted in the 35sq km (13½sq mile) park, and some surviving architectural elements restored. *Qinghua Xi, Haidian District, northwestern suburbs. Tel: (010) 6255 1488. Open: 7am–7pm. Admission charge. Metro: Wudaokou.*

Zhonglou/Gulou (Bell and Drum Towers)

These two edifices lie on the geomantically auspicious north–south line that bisects both the Forbidden City and Tiananmen Square, just to the east of Houhai (Houhai Lake). Originally built as the centre of the capital of the Mongol Yuan Dynasty, the towers were relocated during the Ming era to their present position on the 'dragon's spine'. They have been reconstructed after various depredations (including by Western soldiers during the Boxer Rebellion), but they always served to announce the time, specifically the morning call for all palace functionaries to be at their stations. It's interesting to climb both towers, not just to view the historic bell and the drums, but for a good view into the traditional neighbourhoods below the towers. *Dianmenwai. Tel: (010) 6401 2647. Open: 8am–5pm. Admission charge. Metro: Guloudajie.*

Bike tour: Beijing

Because of the city's size, and the difficulties associated with public transport, the bicycle may be the most practical way of touring Beijing. Special cycle lanes make it generally safe, but great caution must be exercised at intersections and on roads without special lanes. An additional consideration is to secure the bike when you leave it.

Allow 2 hours for this tour; longer if you want to explore the various locations en route.

Begin at the intersection of Xinjiekou Bei and Deshengmen Dong, then turn on to the Xihaibeiyan path along the north bank of Xihai Lake.

1 Xihai (Xihai Lake)

This is the first in a series of lakes stretching southeast towards the city centre, forming a pleasant open space surrounded by *hutongs*. Local people come here to fish and, compared with most of Beijing's public places, these lakes have a wild and ragged look that makes them all the more attractive.
Cross Deshengmennei and join the Houhaibeiyan pathway along the north shore of Houhai Lake.

2 Houhai (Houhai Lake)

The tree-lined, rutted lakeside pathway is a bustle of *hutong* life and colour: students heading for class, street traders, housewives with fresh fruit and vegetables, pungent cooking smells and throngs of cyclists. Heavier traffic generally avoids this lane.
Cross the stone bridge to the Qianhaibeiyan pathway along the western shore of Qianhai Lake, past the He Hua Shi Chang (Lotus Flower street market). Then cross Dianmen Xi and stop at the entrance to Beihai Gongyuan (Beihai Park).

3 Beihai Gongyuan (Beihai Park)

Bicycles are not permitted in the park, so leave yours at the stalls outside and explore the park on foot. This was formerly a playground of China's ruling women, favoured by the Dowager Empress Cixi, and by Jiang Qing, wife of Chairman Mao. Its highlights are Jade Islet and the White Pagoda.

The entrance to Beihai Park

Return to Dianmen Xi and collect your bike. Cycle east a short way before turning right into the narrow lane through Gongjian Hutong.

4 Gongjian Hutong

This offers a fascinating glimpse of Beijing as it used to be, away from the crowded apartment blocks taking over elsewhere. These small, tumbledown houses have an almost rural air.

Emerging on Jingshan Xi, take this narrow, busy road between Beihai Park and Jingshan Park, then on to Beichang, then Nanchang. Turn left into Tiananmen Guangchang (Tiananmen Square).

5 Zijin Cheng (Forbidden City)

Tiananmen Gate, with its giant portrait of Chairman Mao, stands on the left, and through the gate is the entrance to the Forbidden City. This colossal monument to the glories of imperial China is worth an extensive visit, and is best tackled separately if time permits.

Cross over into Tiananmen Square proper. Cycling is not permitted, so you must push your bike across it.

6 Tiananmen Guangchang (Tiananmen Square)

Passing the Renmin Dahui Tang (Great Hall of the People) on your right and the Zhongguo Guojia Bowuguan (National Museum of China) on your left, you arrive across the vast expanse of the square to the Renmin Yingxiong Jinianbei (Monument to the People's Heroes) and the Mao Zhuxi Jinian Tang (Mao Zedong Memorial Hall), where the embalmed body of the late leader is on display.

Exit the square around the monumental Qianmen Gate at its southern end, into Qianmen. Turn left into the hutong district on Zhushikou Dong, then right into Nanqiaowan and Jinyuchizhong, completing your tour at the Tiantan Gongyuan (Temple of Heaven Park).

7 Tiantan Gongyuan (Temple of Heaven Park)

Cycles are not permitted in this monumental park, which was sacred to the emperor as a centre of the state's culture; he would come here every year to pray for a good harvest.

The Forbidden City and Tiananmen Square

Covering 74ha (183 acres) and containing some 800 individual buildings, the scale of the Forbidden City is hard to grasp. It is the most spectacular architectural achievement in the country and it is not surprising that when the Communists took power in 1949, they placed their own ceremonial centre, Tiananmen Square, adjacent to the seat of imperial power.

ZIJIN CHENG (THE FORBIDDEN CITY)

Now officially termed *Gugong* (the Palace Museum), the Forbidden City served for 500 years (until the end of the imperial era in 1911) as the seat of all power in China, the throne of the Son of Heaven, and the private residence of all the Ming and Qing dynasty emperors.

Although it served as residence to 24 emperors for five centuries, the Forbidden City was always far more than a mere palace and visiting this monumental complex is an extraordinary experience. Located in the middle of the capital city of a country that has always called itself the Middle Kingdom, this spot was where, in the minds of the Chinese people, heaven and earth were connected.

Temple lions abound in the Forbidden City

Despite being rebuilt and restored many times throughout the centuries, the structures of the Forbidden City retain the design and, above all, the impressive character of the originals. Begun in 1406 and completed in 1420, construction required the labours of 200,000 workers. The earliest of the completely original structures date to the 18th century, the older structures having been destroyed by the frequent fires to which the wooden buildings were dangerously vulnerable and the ravages of heavy-handed conquerors with a taste for pillage.

Chang'an. Entry is from Tiananmen Square, via the Tiananmen Gate and the Duanmen Gate to the entrance proper,

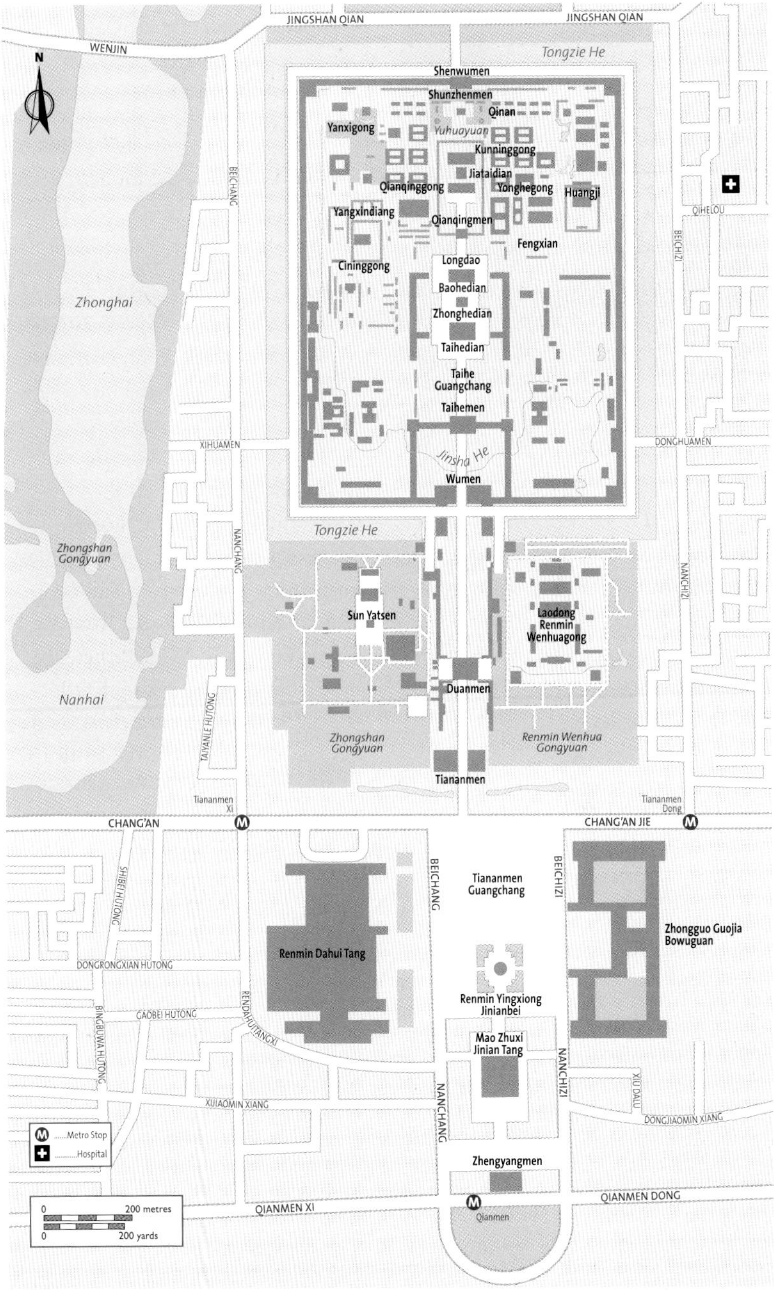
N
JINGSHAN QIAN
JINGSHAN QIAN
WENJIN
Tongzie He
Shenwumen
Shunzhenmen
Qinan
Yuhuayuan
Yanxigong
Kunninggong
Jiataidian
Qianqinggong
Yonghegong
Huangji
Yangxindiang
Qianqingmen
Fengxian
Cininggong
Longdao
Baohedian
Zhonghedian
Taihedian
Taihe
Guangchang
Taihemen
Jinsha He
Wumen
BEICHANG
QIHELOU
BEICHIZI
Zhonghai
XIHUAMEN
DONGHUAMEN
Tongzie He
Zhongshan
Gongyuan
NANCHANG
NANCHIZI
Sun Yatsen
Laodong
Renmin
Wenhuagong
Duanmen
Nanhai
TAIYANLE HUTONG
Zhongshan
Gongyuan
Renmin Wenhua
Gongyuan
Tiananmen
Tiananmen
Xi
Tiananmen
Dong
CHANG'AN
CHANG'AN JIE
SHIBEI HUTONG
BEICHANG
Tiananmen
Guangchang
BEICHIZI
Zhongguo Guojia
Bowuguan
Renmin Dahui Tang
DONGRONGXIAN HUTONG
RENDAHUITANGXI
GAOBEI HUTONG
BINGBUWA HUTONG
Renmin Yingxiong
Jinianbei
Mao Zhuxi
Jinian Tang
NANCHIZI
XIU DALU
XIJIAOMIN XIANG
NANCHANG
DONGJIAOMIN XIANG
......Metro Stop
......Hospital
Zhengyangmen
QIANMEN XI
QIANMEN DONG
Qianmen
0
200 metres
0
200 yards

Tortoise, symbol of longevity

which is at the Meridian Gate (Wumen). Tel: (010) 6513 2255, ext 615. Open: 8.30am–4.30pm (last entry 3.30pm). Admission charge (an excellent taped tour guide to the main locations is available for an extra charge). Metro: Tiananmen Xi or Tiananmen Dong.

Itinerary

The simplest way to tour the Forbidden City is to follow the central axis from south to north, over the **Jinsha He (Golden Stream),** through the **Gate of Supreme Harmony** and across **Taihe Guangchang (Sea of Flagstones)** to the main ceremonial areas in the **Hall of Supreme Harmony**, the **Hall of Complete Harmony** and the **Hall of Preserving Harmony**. Cross **Longdao (Dragon Pavement)** to the imperial family's private domain, through the **Gate of Heavenly Purity**, to the **Palace of Heavenly Purity**, the **Hall of Union** and the **Palace of Earthly Tranquillity**. Cross the **Imperial Gardens** to the **Hall of Imperial Peace** and the **Gate of Obedience and Purity**, exiting through the **Gate of Divine Prowess.** Along this principal route, visits can be made to the numerous side palaces and pavilions, many of which have been laid out as galleries and museums.

Wumen (Meridian Gate)

This powerful defensive tower was built to guard the entrance to the Forbidden City. Today, it is where you buy your ticket to enter the main complex.

Taihemen (Gate of Supreme Harmony)

This gate divides the ornamental outer courtyard, with its Golden Stream, from the more formal inner courtyard

LESSER HALLS

The principal south–north route through the Forbidden City tells only part of the story of this magnificent palace complex. Almost as impressive are the halls and gardens designed for day-to-day affairs of state and for the imperial family's 'everyday life'. Branching off to the east side, you will find several libraries and museums (including the Museum of Art Works Through the Dynasties), and numerous other palaces, pavilions and gardens (including Chengqiangong (the Palace of Eternal Harmony), Fengxian (the Hall of Worshipping Ancestors) and Huangji (the Hall of Imperial Supremacy)). On the western side is another section of the Museum of Art Works Through the Dynasties, as well as the Yanxigong (the Palace of Prolonged Happiness), Yangxindiang (Hall of Mental Cultivation), Cininggong (the Palace of Peace and Tranquillity) and the Hall of Heroic Splendour.

of the Forbidden City's ceremonial section. The courtyard beyond the gate could accommodate up to 100,000 people for imperial audiences.

Taihedian (Hall of Supreme Harmony)

The most substantial of the official pavilions (28m/92ft high), this was also known as the Gold Throne Hall, and was used for important state occasions, for meetings with senior ministers, and for celebrating the emperor's birthday. Incense burners stand before the entrance, one in the shape of a stork, and another in the shape of a dragon; both were auspicious symbols to an emperor. Numerous less ornate burners surround the building. Yellow tiles line the roof of the double-eaved structure, and rows of mythical animals exquisitely rendered in miniature face the corners. The tiled floor and gold painted columns entwined with carved dragons are surmounted by a green and gold painted ceiling, littered with dragon motifs, from which hangs a spherical mirror. Beyond the Hall of Supreme Harmony's tourist-mobbed splendour, you must try to picture the majestic court rituals that took place here: the kowtowing courtiers in splendid robes, clouds of incense smoke and, above all, the august figure of the emperor himself, presiding from the fantastically ornate Dragon Throne.

Zhonghedian (Hall of Complete Harmony)

Somewhat less formal than the Hall of Supreme Harmony and the Hall of Preserving Harmony, this elegant little

The Forbidden City is a vast complex of individual buildings and wide-open courtyards

square hall was used by the emperor as a resting point, and as a place for practising ceremonial speeches. The dragons painted on the ceiling would have reminded officials that 'relaxation' was a relative term in the emperor's presence. Qing Dynasty sedans, used for transporting the emperor around the palace, are on display.

Baohedian (Hall of Preserving Harmony)

Highly decorated, and with ornate ceilings and beams, this graceful hall was used for imperial banquets, as a changing room for the emperor before official ceremonies, and as an examination centre for candidates for senior positions within the imperial bureaucracy. Behind the hall, a giant slab of marble, weighing more than 200 tonnes (197 tons), is inscribed with dragon and cloud motifs.

A censer for burning incense

Qianqingmen (Gate of Heavenly Purity)

This marks the entrance to the inner sanctum, the palace area of the Forbidden City, which was accessible only to members of the imperial family.

Qianqinggong (Palace of Heavenly Purity)

Until the early 18th century, the emperors slept in this palace at the centre of the inner courtyard. After they withdrew to the Hall of Mental Cultivation, it was used to receive foreign ambassadors.

Jiataidian (Hall of Union)

A water clock, or clepsydra, graces this small building, also known as the Hall of Vigorous Fertility. Here, the empress held court when the hall was used as living quarters by the imperial family.

Kunninggong (Palace of Earthly Tranquillity)

During the Qing Dynasty, this was the official residence of the empress, and the bedchamber for the imperial couple for several days following their nuptials. The garish red decoration of the chamber put at least one emperor off his wedding-night ritual, so he and his new wife moved back to their permanent apartments.

The Gate of Supreme Harmony

Yuhuayuan (Imperial Gardens)

Located north of the Gate of Earthly Tranquillity, and around the Hall of Imperial Peace, the Imperial Garden seems surprisingly small – at least in comparison with the grandiose scale of the palace complex. Nevertheless, it covers some 7,000sq m (75,320sq ft) in the classical Chinese garden style. Its impressive rock formations, pools and plant-bedecked spaces form a notable and suitably tranquil hideaway.

The foot-weary visitor will no doubt welcome a chance to rest here in the shade before leaving the Forbidden City through the Gate of Divine Prowess (Shenwumen, also translated as the 'Gate of Divine Military Genius'), which stands at the northern end of the complex.

TIANANMEN SQUARE

Tiananmen Guangchang (Tiananmen Square)

Laid out in 1959, Beijing's vast central square has witnessed gatherings of up to a million people, including the cheering throngs who greeted Chairman Mao's pronouncements during the Cultural Revolution. Since 1989, its name has been irrevocably associated with the pro-democracy demonstrations that ended in the wanton killings of students by the army and the subsequent suppression of the survivors. Mostly, however, it is a tranquil location to stroll in and watch people flying their kites. At its southern end is the **Monument to the People's Heroes**, a 36m (118ft) high granite

obelisk decorated with revolutionary images and calligraphy by Chairman Mao. The two large buildings on the east side of the square are museums that are closed for renovation and scheduled to reopen in 2009.
Located immediately south of the Forbidden City.

Tiananmen (Gate of Heavenly Peace)

Tiananmen Gate or the Gate of Heavenly Peace dates from 1417 and was restored in 1651 after being burnt down by rebels. Today its giant portrait of Chairman Mao is a familiar backdrop in images of the capital. It was from atop this gate that Mao proclaimed the founding of the People's Republic of China on 1 October 1949, and addressed the 'Red Guards' during the Cultural Revolution. This is the entrance to the Imperial City (although not to the moat-encircled Forbidden City proper), and only the emperor was permitted to use the central one of its five gates.
North end of Tiananmen Square.
Tel: (010) 6513 2255, ext 615.
Open: 8.30am–4.30pm. Admission charge to climb to the top of the gate. Free admission through the gate as far as the main entrance to the Forbidden City.

The Meridian Gate in the Forbidden City

Sections of the Forbidden City – silent reminders of a splendid past

Mao Zhuxi Jinian Tang (Mao Zedong Memorial Hall)

Chairman Mao, the late Great Helmsman of the People's Republic and leader of the Chinese Revolution, is embalmed here in a crystal sarcophagus, despite his publicly stated wishes to avoid any manifestations of a personality cult. The building itself, situated to face Tiananmen Gate, is an example of the Socialist Realism style imported from the Soviet Union. Mao continues to command respect – despite the disasters he wrought, the official claim that Mao was 70 per cent good and only 30 per cent bad still carries weight, and the Chinese people, although in lessening numbers, still pass respectfully by his casket.

South side of Tiananmen Square. Tel: (010) 6513 2277. Open: Mon, Wed, Fri 8.30–11.30am, 2–4pm, Tue, Thur, Sat & Sun 8.30–11.30am. Free admission. No cameras or bags allowed.

Renmin Dahui Tang (Great Hall of the People)

China's parliament meets in this 1950s vintage edifice once a year in March to consider the decisions of the Politburo and Central Committee with great care, before approving them. A guided tour offers a glimpse of the style that the people's tribunes have grown accustomed to, including a 5,000-place banqueting hall.

West side of Tiananmen Square. Tel: (010) 6309 6156. Open: 8.30am–2pm, except when official events are taking place inside. Admission charge.

The imperial court

Beijing had its first taste of imperial glory in the 10th century as a secondary capital. Kublai Khan made it the primary capital in AD 1279. Then, after a period during which Nanjing was the main city, Beijing again became the capital under the Ming Emperor Yongle in AD 1420. From then until 1911, throughout the Ming and Qing dynasties, the extravagance and power of the imperial court were still maintained in Beijing – the focal point of the Chinese empire. Ensconced in the Forbidden City, the Son of Heaven became completely isolated, not only from his people, whom he viewed through a screen of Confucian duties, rituals and displays of loyalty (and occasionally of rebellion), but often from reality itself. Throughout the Age of Enlightenment and the scientific revolution that was transforming Europe, China remained locked in a social system more appropriate to antiquity than to a great but now weakened empire, threatened by predatory foreign powers.

Secrets of the Qing court

The imperial court attained the height of its splendour during the Qing period, especially under the emperors Kangxi (1662–1722) and his grandson, Qianlong (1735–96). These emperors may have been considered the all-powerful Sons of Heaven, but their court lives were subject to a rigorous discipline. At meal times, the emperor would eat alone in his private quarters – breakfast at dawn, lunch at midday and dinner at sunset. All food was carefully prepared in the imperial kitchen and he would be served eight main dishes, four side dishes, three accompanying types of soup, and assorted sweets, cakes, buns and, of course, rice. Before eating, a court eunuch would taste each dish to ensure it had not been poisoned. Only the finest ingredients were fit for the emperor's table, and since he could not possibly consume everything set before him with such regularity, the very substantial leftovers were passed down to his concubines, eunuchs and court officials – this was considered a symbol of great privilege.

After dinner, the emperor would prepare to retire to bed. An appropriate concubine had already been chosen during the course of the day, and had spent the afternoon being prepared for the imperial bedchamber. Soon after the emperor had retired, the concubine would be led to the emperor by a court eunuch, but she was never permitted to spend the entire night in the imperial presence, being admitted to a smaller side chamber after conjugal union had taken place. Court eunuchs kept a careful record of which concubines had slept with the emperor and when, since the purpose of these unions was not primarily the emperor's sexual satisfaction, but the procreation of the imperial line through as many male heirs as possible.

Kowtowing time

On a visit to the Forbidden City, it takes considerable effort to shut out the noise of the chattering crowds and to try to imagine the scene at one of the great court ceremonies of the past. The red walls and yellow-tiled roofs would then have been veiled by swirling curtains of smoke from incense burners. Hosts of silk-clad officials would be kowtowing – kneeling with forehead touching the ground – as the emperor was carried in his palanquin to his magnificent throne. In the background the 10,000 eunuchs and 9,000 ladies-in-waiting that the palace boasted at the height of its power would be gathered. Such ceremonies continued to take place unchanged for five centuries, throughout the reigns of 24 emperors. Meanwhile, the world had changed, and Communism finally ruled in the imperial court. Whether they be antiquarians or tourists, Chinese or foreigners, all observers can be thankful that the people's government has finally opened the door to this venerable setting of Chinese mystery and intrigue.

Looking towards the Meridian Gate

Beijing environs

Surrounding Beijing are several sights worth a visit not only for their historical significance, but also as an oasis of calm after time spent in the city. Apparently the emperors agreed with this analysis for this is where they built their own pleasure palaces and gardens to escape Beijing's heat and noise, as well as palace intrigue, and importuning noblemen and officials.

In areas deemed to possess auspicious *feng shui,* the emperors and their families chose their final resting places. Both the Ming and the Qing emperors built their tombs in three sites outside the capital. Further afield, but still close enough to do as a day trip from Beijing, lies the city of Tianjin, which was the home of foreign merchants during the late 19th and early 20th centuries. Their legacy remains in architecture – some splendid old churches and other Western structures dot the city.

Biyun Si (Temple of Azure Clouds)

Adjacent to Fragrant Hills Park, Biyun Si contains **Wubai Luohan Tang (Hall of Five Hundred Arhats)** (508 representations of the Buddha), as well as a memorial to the Chinese nationalist leader Sun Yatsen. **Jingangbaozuo Ta (Diamond Throne Pagoda)** is surrounded by four smaller pagodas.
Xi Shan (Western Hills). Tel: (010) 6259 1155. Open: 8am–5pm (until sunset in summer). Admission charge. Can be reached by bus from the Summer Palace.

Qing Dong Ling (Eastern Qing tombs)

These are the most attractive of the imperial tombs near Beijing. The route to the tombs passes through interesting countryside, and the area of the tombs offers pleasant streams running through a forest, and a backdrop of mountains. Stone gates, marble bridges and a 'spirit way' lined by sculptures similar to that at the Ming Tombs (*see pp57–8*) all combine to create a good cultural experience.

Among the notables entombed here are the Emperor Qianlong and the notorious Dowager Empress Cixi. Altogether there are the tombs of 5 emperors, 14 empresses and 130 or so other relations of the imperial families. The tombs of Qianlong and Cixi, although looted during the 1920s, still contain much of interest in the way of carvings, inscriptions and other decorations. Qianlong, whose 60-year reign was the longest of the dynasty's 10 rulers, had a masssive underground tomb built for himself prior to his demise. The interior of the tomb is covered with bas-reliefs of both Buddhist and Taoist deities, as well as statuary and inscriptions in both Tibetan and Sanskrit. Qianlong wanted to cover all his bases, even in the afterlife.

As would be expected, the grandest of the tombs is that of the Dowager Empress Cixi. Since she expired before the edifice was completed, and could therefore not command its completion, it is the exterior portions that contain the most elaborately carved stonework. At the nearby Hall of Eminent Favours, a museum exhibits Cixi's daily-use items, including ceremonial robes and articles placed within her tomb.

Zunhua County, 128km (79½ miles) east of Beijing, close to the Great Wall. Open: 8.30am–5pm. Admission charge.

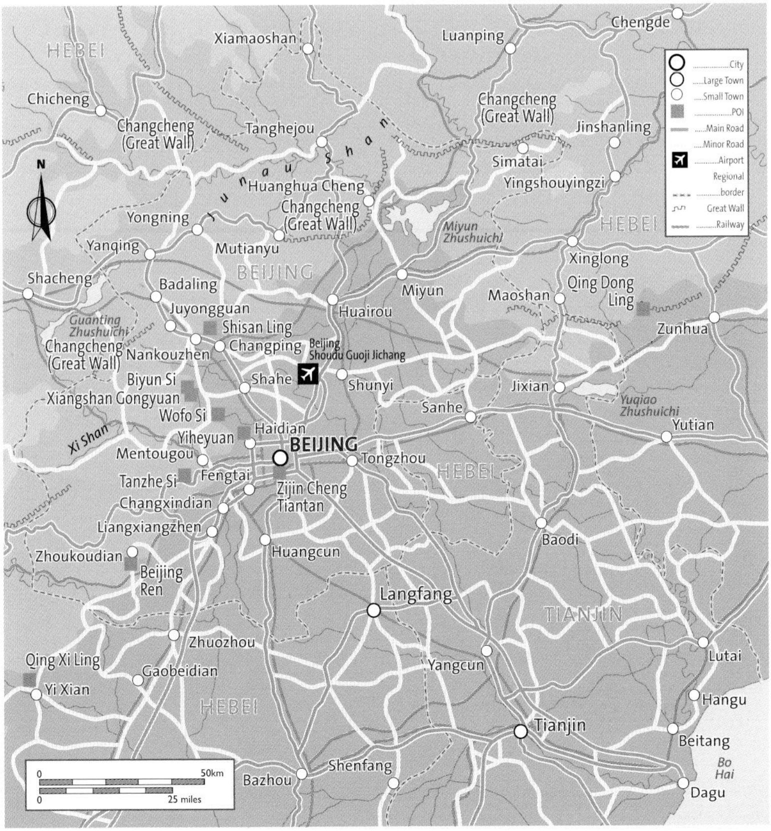

Chinese medicine

During the Ming Dynasty, female herbalists – reputed to be witches – from Guizhou Province in Southwest China are said to have concocted a wicked brew that could entrap men in matrimony. Today, most herbalists are engaged in the far less sinister task of trying to cure the everyday afflictions of the human condition such as haemorrhoids, impotence, insomnia, eczema and even old age.

Guizhou remains at the centre of the Chinese medical world and is the source of many medicinal plants that grow abundantly in its hills, forming the basic ingredients of a medical revolution. One product is a cure for haemorrhoids that involves dissolving a herbal powder in water and sitting in it for 30 minutes while the problem vanishes. It seems too good to be true, and it probably is, yet the market for this and other cures is booming. One company reportedly makes around US$30 million a year selling herbal sperm regeneration powders and herbal aphrodisiacs, while it is playing the other side of the procreation market by trying to develop a herbal contraceptive.

As in all traditional societies, herbalists and alternative practitioners use a variety of ingredients to effect their cures

An old medicine shop in the Qianmen area of Beijing

The alternative way to health

Traditional Chinese medicine has a 2,000-year legacy and is favoured by a quarter of humanity for its supposed efficacy. The first official pharmacopoeia was produced in AD 659. New 'traditional' medicines are being added to the doctor's armoury all the time. Unfortunately, some of the alternative medicines rely heavily on animal products. Today, organisations like World Wide Fund for Nature (WWF) are working with traditional Chinese medicine practitioners to encourage them not to use the bones and horns of endangered species such as tigers and rare deer. Acupuncture, in which needles are inserted at key nerve centres in the skin, and reflexology are among the better-known techniques and are said to be effective against a wide range of conditions, including rheumatism, travel sickness and the common cold.

Chronic ailments are often treated with herbal remedies, said to have fewer side-effects than Western-style drugs, and simple complaints like colds can be ameliorated in the same way. For acute conditions, especially those requiring surgery, modern techniques are likely to be more reliable.

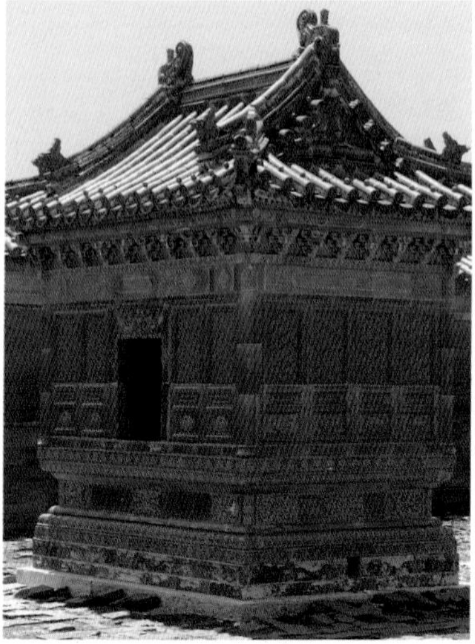

The Sacred Silk Burner of Emperor Qianlong in the Eastern Qing Tombs

Qing Xi Ling (Western Qing Tombs)

The western burial ground of the Manchu Qing Dynasty emperors (1644–1911), who overthrew the Ming Dynasty, lies in the shadow of 1,121m (3,678ft) high Yunmeng Mountain in rugged countryside 112km (69½ miles) southwest of Beijing, across the border in Hebei Province. Because of its distance from the capital and lack of other significant sights of interest nearby, the Western Qing Tombs are much less visited than the other royal tomb sites.

This necropolis was started by Emperor Yongzheng (reigned 1723–35) as an alternative to the site used by earlier Qing emperors. It is theorised that he did not wish to be laid to rest next to his father, whose will he had ignored in usurping the throne from his brother, the designated heir. Yongzheng continued to eliminate rivals, by execution or exile, throughout his reign.

Five Qing emperors are interred here, as well as three empresses and many princes and royal concubines. The last Qing monarch to die as an emperor, Guangxu, is buried here, but the true last emperor, the ill-fated boy emperor Pu Yi, is buried in a public cemetery nearby. He was made a puppet ruler subservient to the Japanese during World War II, and

THE OPIUM WARS

China was forcibly opened to the world by the British in the aftermath of the Opium Wars of 1839–42 and 1856–60. Concerned that the profits of trade, in particular tea, were flowing too much in China's favour, Britain aimed to reverse this process by forcing opium grown in India on the Chinese. China protested against the 'foreign mud' that was turning its people into addicts, so Britain sent warships to protect the drug barons' interests. China fought back and lost.

While most of the activity took place in the south of China, farther from the central government's authority, foreign troops during the Second Opium War sacked Beijing and looted priceless artefacts before destroying what they could not take. Both of Beijing's summer palaces were nearly reduced to rubble, and Tianjin was effectively ceded to foreigners.

While individual Chinese bear no ill-will to foreigners for these acts – they've seen far worse, under the Japanese and, some would say, indigenous overlords – the Chinese government never tires of mentioning this humiliating chapter in China's history, especially when lectured about human rights.

later a common worker during Communist rule.

Beyond the town of Yi Xian.
Open: 8am–5pm. Admission charge.

Shisan Ling (Ming Tombs)

There are 13 Ming Dynasty imperial tombs in this 40sq km (15½sq mile) necropolis, situated at the base of the optimistically named Mountain of Heavenly Longevity. Built between 1409 and 1644, only three of the tombs are open to the public and only one, the tomb of Emperor Wanli (Dingling), the 13th Ming emperor, has been fully excavated and laid out for visitors. The sites that have not been restored and their surrounding buildings, as well as the tombs of those other than emperors, such as concubines, have the advantage of being less crowded.

The architectural attractions here are not, however, the tombs themselves, but the surrounding halls where the living came to commemorate their ancestors. Outside the tomb of Emperor Yongli (Changling) is **Lingendian (Hall of Eminent Favour)**, one of the best existing examples of Ming Dynasty architecture in China. Built on a three-level marble terrace, this twin-eaved structure is supported by massive fragrant cedar columns. The hall is now a museum that exhibits treasures retrieved from the excavated tombs, particularly that of Emperor Wanli, whose tomb was opened by archaeologists in the 1950s, and was one of the few to escape tomb robbers.

The Way of Stone figures at the Ming Tombs

Other items on display were retrieved from unscrupulous antiquities dealers who acquired them from tomb robbers.

The tombs are reached via the 7km (4½-mile) Shendao (Way of the Spirit), whose first 750m (820yds), called the Way of Stone Figures, is guarded by two lines of fascinating stone animals (some of them mythical) and human servants of the emperor, all indicating respect for and loyalty to their departed master. *Located 50km (31 miles) northwest of Beijing. Often combined with a visit to the Great Wall. Tel: (010) 6976 1424. Open: 8am–5.30pm. Admission charge.*

BEIJING REN (PEKING MAN)

Some 580,000 years ago, the area around the town of Zhoukoudian (50km/31 miles southwest of Beijing), was occupied by a species of early proto-humans whom palaeontologists have named Peking Man (*Sinanthropus pekininsis*). Local residents often found 'dragon bones', as they called the fossils, in a limestone cavern on Longgushan (Dragon Bone Mountain). The first intact fragment, a skull (which disappeared in World War II), was discovered in 1929. Since then, fragments of 40 other 'man-apes' have been uncovered in various locations nearby.

Tanzhe Si (Tanzhe Temple)

Dating from the 3rd century AD, this huge Buddhist temple, Beijing's largest, sprawls across Mentougou's Western Hills. It is particularly famous for its very old cypress and pine trees. Within the grounds, a collection of old stupas contains the remains of famous monks. *Mentougou District, 45km (28 miles) west of Beijing. Tel: (010) 6086 2505. Open: 8.30am–6pm. Admission charge.*

Hall of Eminent Favour, Shisan Ling

Tianjin

Tianjin is China's fourth largest city (10 million population) and one of the four independent municipalities (besides Beijing, Shanghai and Chongqing) that are part of no province and thus have more influence than other cities. It is connected to the sea by the Hai River, and is the closest port city to Beijing. Indeed, it can be reached in 90 minutes by a comfortable express train from the capital city. During the late 19th century, Tianjin was one of the treaty ports where foreign merchants were allowed to settle and do business, and interesting examples of Western architecture remain, especially hotels, schools, banks and churches. While doubtlessly living in the shadow of nearby Beijing, Tianjin is proud of its independence and has several attractions for the visitor. Apart from the concession-era Western architecture, there are Buddhist and Confucian temples, Gu Wenhua Jie (Ancient Culture Street), and an interesting antiques market.

Dabeiyuan (Dabei Monastery)

In the north of the city centre, the Dabei Monastery is dedicated to the Maitreya, the Buddha of the Coming Age, or what is known to Westerners as the Laughing Buddha. To the Chinese, his rotund shape is not obesity but represents an accumulation of wisdom. The temple also houses an image of the Goddess of Mercy, Guanyin – a female incarnation of the Buddha. The area surrounding this Qing Dynasty era temple is an interesting old neighbourhood, with many shops selling votive items such as incense.
40 Tianwei Lu, Dabeiyuan. Tel: (022) 2626 1769. Open: 9am–4.30pm. Admission charge.

Ornate decoration on a Ming tomb

Gu Wenhua Jie (Ancient Culture Street)

In the centre of the downtown area of the city, there is a recent but nonetheless interesting recreation of a traditional Chinese urban marketplace. Aimed at tourists, both Chinese and foreign, the shops here sell the standard Chinoiserie, from scroll paintings to Mao memorabilia. To live up to the 'culture' part of its name, the authorities dispatch troupes of wandering musicians who play in the streets. At Spring Festival, full Beijing Opera performances are scheduled.

Jiefang Lu

On Jiefang Lu, directly behind the hotel, head north and you will pass a veritable museum of old concession-period architecture. The structures were originally banks built by the likes of Jardine Matheson (one of the original opium importers) and Citibank, although both the Germans and the Japanese had major operations here. The structures are both opulent and grandiose, and after a period of disrepute and decay during the Communist era, they are now being restored, and are occupied by Chinese banks, who now dance to the capitalist music.

Lishunde Fandian (Astor Hotel)

Constructed by foreigners during the period when Tianjin was a treaty port is the Astor Hotel, located along the bank of the Hai River, which runs through the middle of the city. This hotel was originally owned by a British firm in the late 19th century, and was frequented by none other than the last emperor of China, Pu Yi, when he was exiled from Beijing by the republican government in 1925. Pu Yi lived in Tianjin with his empress and a concubine until the Japanese invaded China in 1937. A collection of old photographs of notables who visited the hotel is on display in a hall adjacent to the lobby.

33 Tai'erzhuang Lu.

Tel: (022) 2331 1688.

Open: Daily. Free admission.

Tianhou Goug (Tianhou Temple)

Adjacent to the Ancient Culture Street lies the much less commercial and more tranquil Tianhou Temple, a Buddhist temple commemorating Mazu, the

Dried flowers and herbs used for infusions for sale at Tianjin's market

View towards the Fragrant Hills

goddess of the sea, which befits Tianjin's traditional role as Northern China's largest port city. The temple was originally constructed during the 14th-century Yuan Dynasty, and attracts a large number of worshippers.
Gu Wenhua Jie. Tel: (022) 2727 5062. Open: 9am–5pm. Admission charge.

Xikai Jiaotang (Xikai Cathedral)
Further west, on Nanjing Lu, this is another relic of the concession era. Opened by the French in 1916, this is the biggest of Tianjin's several Christian places of worship and is filled with local Catholics on Sundays.
Dushan Lu. Tel: (022) 2835 8812. Open: 7.30am–8pm. Free admission.

Zhongxin Gongyuan (Zhongxin Park)
A few blocks west of these buildings, on the corner of Heping Lu and Chifeng Dao, Zhongxin Park is a large circular garden surrounded by Western architecture which momentarily transports the visitor to Europe.

Wofo Si (Temple of the Reclining Buddha)
Also known as the Temple of Universal Spiritual Awakening, this building takes its name from the statue of the reclining or sleeping Buddha that it contains. Dating from 1331, it is the largest bronze statue in the country, more than 5m (16½ft) long and weighing 54 tonnes (53 tons).
Located between the Fragrant Hills and the Summer Palace. Tel: (010) 6259 1155. Open: 8am–4.30pm. Admission charge.

Xiangshan Gongyuan (Fragrant Hills)
Near the Summer Palace (*see pp62–5*) this 150ha (370-acre) park is a great

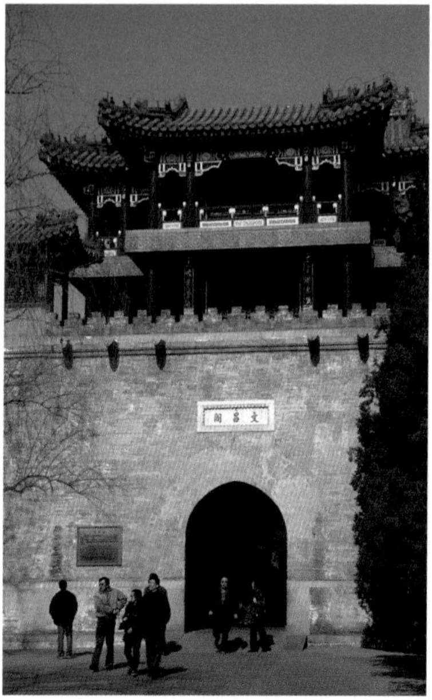

The entrance gate of the Summer Palace

respite from the city, but be forewarned: on fine weekend days it will be jam-packed with people. A good time to visit is in the autumn, when the sycamore tree's leaves turn a brilliant red. If you want to savour the atmosphere, there is a splendid hotel (Xiangshan Hotel) designed by the famous Chinese-American architect I M Pei within the park grounds.

Once a favoured retreat of emperors and the noble classes who had second homes here, it reached its peak of popularity during the Qing Dynasty under Emperor Qianlong when it was known as the Garden of Tranquillity and Charm. The area is peppered with temples, pagodas and pavilions, including the ruined **Xiangshan Si (Fragrant Hill Temple)**, which was razed by British and French troops during the Second Opium War, the magnificent **Zhaomiao (Luminous Temple)** with its **Liulita (Glazed Tile Pagoda)**, and **Banshanting (Villa of Climbing to Clouds)**. A chair lift travels to the summit of **Xianglu Feng (Incense Burner Peak)**, which gives a splendid view of the area.

Yiheyuan (Summer Palace)

The most magnificent of all China's royal gardens, the Summer Palace is an eloquent testimony to imperial power. The term 'Summer Palace' is something of a misnomer created by foreigners – in fact, many emperors spent most of the year here. The notorious Dowager Empress Cixi loved her pleasure gardens dearly and created some of the most opulent structures found in China here. Although it was originally created during the Ming Dynasty, it was designed in its current form by the Qing Emperor Qianlong, who reigned from 1736 to 1795. It is, however, the Qing Dowager Empress Cixi who is most irrevocably linked to the palace since she had it restored twice during her reign, once in 1860 after it was plundered by British and French troops during the Second Opium War, and again in 1902 when foreign troops sought reprisals for the Boxer Rebellion, an anti-Christian movement.

The Chinese name for the Summer Palace, Yiheyuan, literally means 'Garden of Cultivated Harmony'. The design elements are worthy of the name as the atmosphere here, while appearing natural, is quite well planned. Open pavilions are situated to best appreciate specific views, and an intricate system of walled courtyards reveals the landscape in incremental segments, rather like viewing a series of framed paintings. The palace has extensive wooded areas as well as temples, fanciful shrines and large residential buildings and ceremonial halls. The entire walled complex covers an area of 290ha (716 acres).

Although the palace is designed to create a microcosm of nature, with hills, elaborate rock gardens and water features, water is the principal motif, forming **Kunming Lake** in the process. The lake covers over half the entire complex and is covered by lotus blossoms in the summer months. Three small islands dot the lake, each with its own secluded pavilion. Passenger boats now ply the lake, giving visitors a view of the palace complex.

The **Changlang (Long Corridor)**, stretching for 700m (765yds) along the northern shore of Kunming Lake, commands superb views over the water and up to **Wanshou Shan (Longevity Hill)**. The interior is decorated with over 14,000 restored paintings of scenes from Chinese history. The Long Corridor leads to **Qingyanfang (The Marble Boat)** of Cixi. This odd structure, which is in fact neither marble nor a boat, is known to all Chinese as a symbol of Empress Cixi's frivolity in the face of foreign threats. Allegedly using funds budgeted to build a modern navy, Cixi instead squandered the money on this odd structure. Soon

The Marble Boat

The Long Corridor

after, the Japanese crushed the outmoded Chinese navy.

Wanshou Shan (Longevity Hill), located north of Kunming Lake, is studded with temples, pavilions and pagodas. At its base lies **Baoyun ge Tongdian (Bronze Pavilion)**, a 188-tonne (207-ton) structure constructed entirely of this metal but in a surprisingly realistic imitation of timber. A plethora of structures dot the hill, including the **Paiyundian (Temple of Scattering Clouds)**, **Foxiangge (Temple of Buddhist Virtue)**, **Zhihuihi (Temple of Wisdom)**, **Dehuidian (Hall of Virtuous Light)** and the **Zhuanlunzang (Repository of Sutras)**. Longevity Hill and its various sights can become quite crowded during peak times, so try to get here early or save it until the end of your visit.

To the east of Longevity Hill, **Deheyuan (Garden of Virtue and Harmony)** is an amazing three-level theatre where Beijing Opera performances were given for Cixi's pleasure. The three levels were used to represent the heavens, from which celestial beings would descend to the middle level of mortals, while the bottom level was home to the demons. Today, the theatre is a museum displaying not only costumes and other items used in the opera performances but also some of Cixi's royal regalia. Cixi observed the performances from the still displayed magnificent gilded throne in the adjacent **Yiledian (Hall of Cultivating Happiness)**.

One of the more tranquil areas of the Summer Palace is **Xiequyuan (Garden of Harmonious Pleasures)** near the East Gate. Designed to replicate a similar structure in the city of Wuxi in Central China, this was Cixi's favourite spot for fishing. It has a lotus pond at the centre, and it was here that the Summer Palace scenes in the film *The Last Emperor* were filmed.

On the southeastern shore of the lake is the graceful **Shiqi Kong Qiao (Seventeen-Arch Bridge)** that crosses to South Lake Island where boats can be boarded to cross the lake to the Marble Boat. At the beginning of the bridges, a large bronze ox statue reposes, a symbol of protection from floods and malevolent water spirits. For extra protection, each of the bridge's 544 balustrades is topped by a marble lion dispelling airborne evil influences.

Haidian District, 10km (6 miles) northwest of Beijing. Tel: (010) 6288 1144. Open: 6.30am–7.30pm (summer); 7am–5pm (winter). Admission charge. An interesting way to reach the Summer Palace (except in winter) is by boat, travelling by canals from the Beijing Aquarium. Alternatively, bus No 707 departs from near the Beijing Zoo.

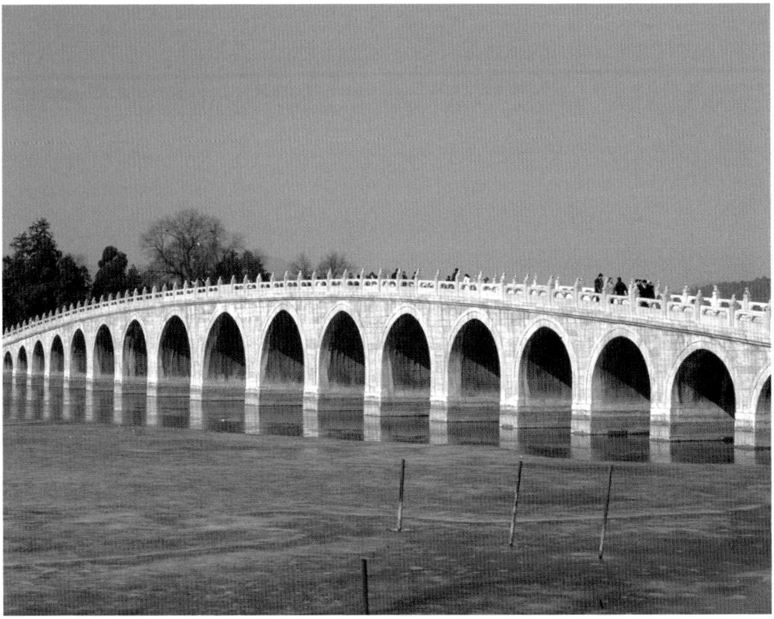

The Seventeen-Arch Bridge on Kunming Lake

Changcheng (The Great Wall)

Not only one of the greatest engineering feats of the ancient world, but also China's best-known icon, the Great Wall is a must-see for every visitor to Beijing. The massive structure epitomises the power and tyranny of ancient China's dynasties as well as their technical prowess, but most importantly it signifies China's ultimately unsuccessful insularity.

The wall's western terminus is a fortress at Jiayuguan in the Gansu Province desert. From there it meanders across deserts and over precipitous mountains for about 4,000km (2,485 miles) to the Yellow Sea at Shanhaiguan in Liaoning Province.

The wall we visit today dates from the 14th-century Ming Dynasty, but the idea of a single protective wall with fortifications was conceived, not unsurprisingly, by the Qin emperor, Qin Shi Huang, who united China under his rule during the Qin Dynasty (221–206 BC). Prior to this, many smaller walls were built by local kingdoms, all seeking protection from the fierce Mongol tribes north of the Yellow River plains. The Qin and earlier walls were built of bricks and rammed earth (as well as, the story goes, the bones of the forced labourers who died during its construction – up to 300,000 labourers toiled for ten years to construct the Qin-era Great Wall). The Ming-era builders covered their wall with stone slabs and added the watchtowers that dot the wall today.

In spite of its impressive appearance, the wall rarely succeeded in protecting China from determined invaders. The Mongols breached the wall in several places during the 11th century and went on to found the Yuan Dynasty with a capital in Beijing. The Manchus swept down from the Northeast to overthrow the Ming in the 17th century. Then, no force was required when the Manchus

The Chinese are enthusiastic tourists in their own country: the Great Wall

benefited from the defection of a Ming general and simply bribed demoralised local sentries into allowing them to pass. Nonetheless, the Great Wall is one of the most popular Chinese symbols of patriotism. It adorns the currency, and the badges of the police.

Much of the wall has fallen into disrepair since the Ming Dynasty, but certain sections have been restored to give both domestic and foreign visitors an idea of what this great structure once entailed. The most regularly visited site is at Badaling, only two hours' drive from Beijing, but those seeking less crowded and commercialised sites can venture to Mutianyu, Juyongguan, Simatai, Jinshanling and Huanghua Cheng.

VISITING THE GREAT WALL

Badaling

It is here that most visitors encounter the Great Wall since it is the closest restored area of the wall to Beijing, only 70km (44 miles) away, about an hour by car.

The scenery is spectacular, but so are crowds, and a visit should not be undertaken on weekends. In addition to the visitors, an army of souvenir vendors camp at the base of the wall and beyond. If you want to sing karaoke or be photographed in Ming robes astride a slightly odoriferous camel, you can be accommodated here.

The restored watchtowers and ramparts afford great views of the wall as it snakes across the mountainous

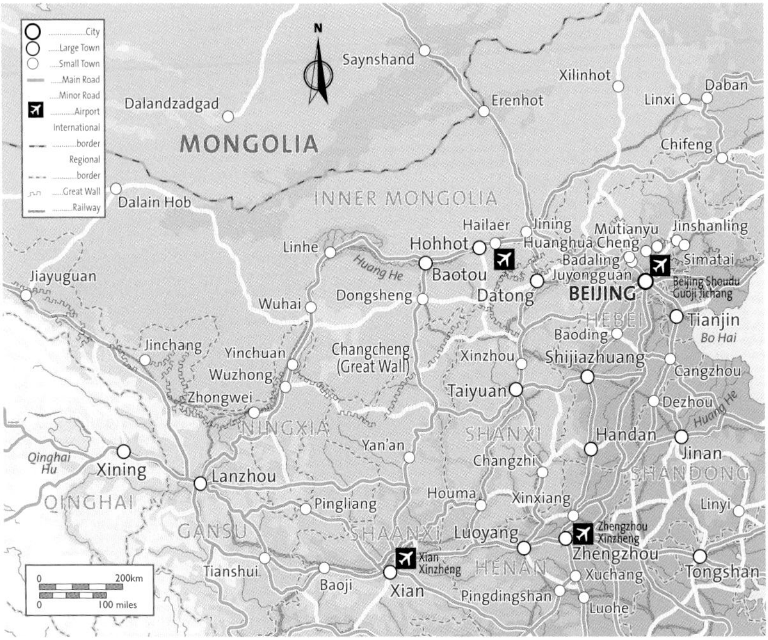

terrain. The climb to the top of the wall is helped by staircases with guard rails, but a cable car also makes the trip. From the top, you can walk along the 6m (20ft) wide wall in either direction, but out-walking the crowds means clambering over sections of the wall that have not been restored. A visit to the **China Great Wall Museum**, which shows a good short film on a 360-degree surround screen, is included in the admission charge.

The trip to the Great Wall at Badaling is often coupled with a visit to the Ming Tombs. This makes a good day's outing, but check in advance that the tour does not include time-consuming diversions to tourist traps such as jade 'factories', gem shops and, worse, Chinese medical clinics where charlatans debase this often useful form of medical treatment by examining busloads of foreign 'patients' and prescribing treatments available for purchase on the spot.

Tel: (010) 6912 1423. Open: 6am–10pm (summer); 7am–6pm (winter). Admission charge.

No public transport, but every tour operator offers this trip – try the Beijing Sightseeing Bus Centre near Tiananmen Square, tel: (010) 8353 1111.

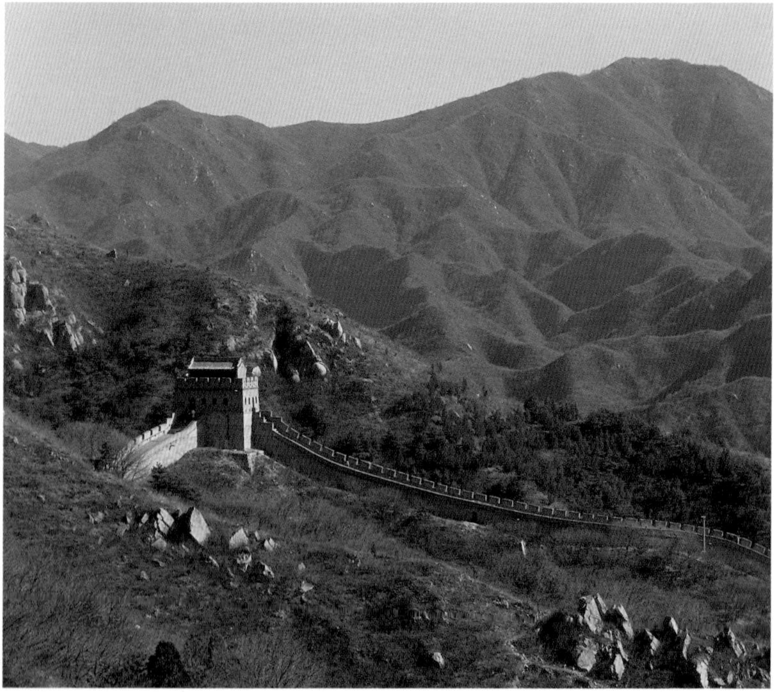

Universally known symbol of China, the Great Wall at Badaling

Huanghua Cheng

Only 60km (40 miles) northeast of Beijing but a world away from the atmosphere of Badaling, this is a rough section of the wall not far from Mutianyu. Although there is a cable car and some of the fortresses have been restored, the pathways at some parts are both steep and slippery – the gravel-like masonry requires proper footwear and your attention. The wall here is bisected by a reservoir, and the surrounding countryside is lush with walnut and chestnut orchards. Some enterprising local residents have started small restaurants and guesthouses near the reservoir, and can be good sources of current information. Restoration (including improvements to the pathways leading to the wall) is in progress.

WALKING THE WALL

A fulfilling trip to the Great Wall can be strenuous because to fully appreciate it you need to get away from the crowds. It's pretty difficult to get lost, but a safe and comfortable trip requires some basic precautions. Be sure to wear shoes that are not only comfortable but have good ankle support and soles that will grip the uneven surfaces in the sections that have not been restored. Be especially careful of loose rock and gravel. The wall is exposed to wind and sometimes rain, so it can go from hot to cold quickly; therefore, wear several layers of clothing topped with a weatherproof shell. Apply sunscreen. Although water and sweets vendors are ubiquitous, make sure you have some water and food with you.

Bactrian camel on the Great Wall, north of Beijing

Open: 8am–5pm. Admission charge. From Beijing, take bus No 961 from the Dongzhimen Long Distance Bus Station.

Juyongguan

On the road to Badaling, about 50km (33 miles) from Beijing, Juyongguan is a good spot to view the Great Wall if you want to avoid the crowds, although admittedly the scenery is not as spectacular as at Badaling. It's a steep climb to the top of the wall and there is no cable car. A good choice if you're short of time and it is a weekend.
For opening hours and transport options, see Badaling, p68.

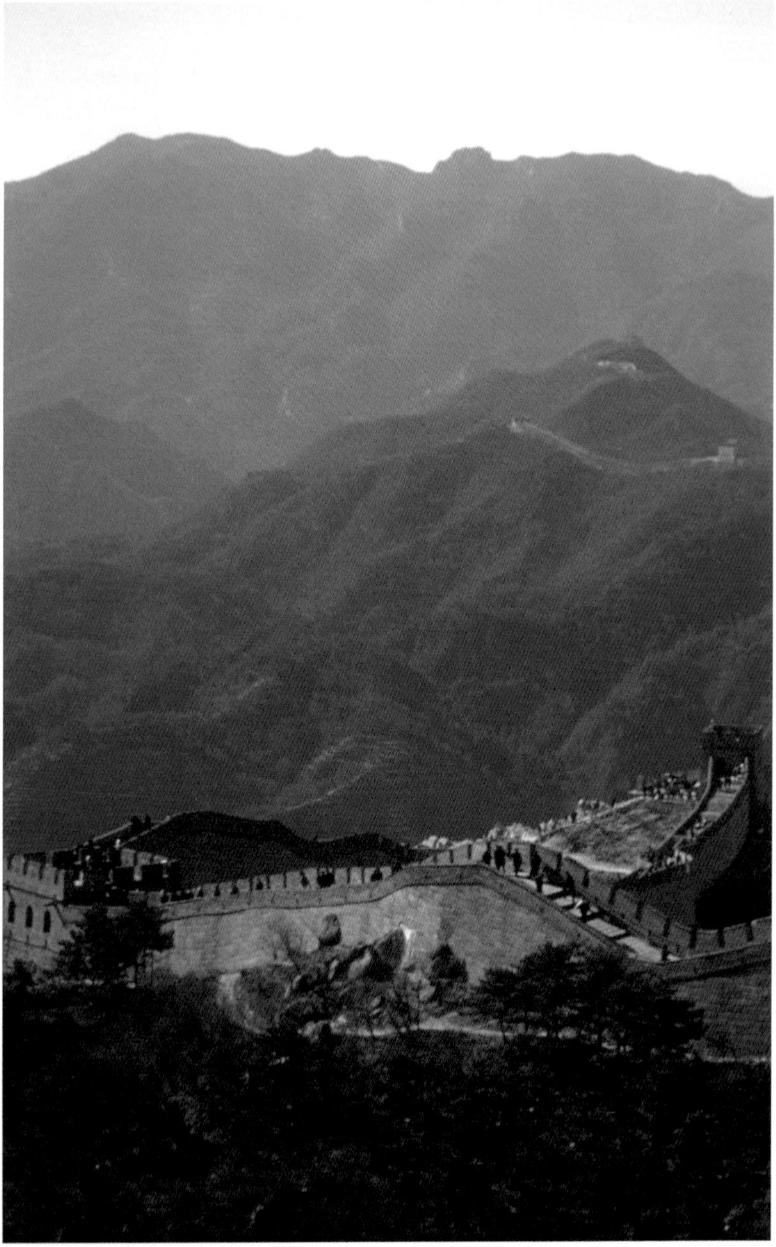

The Great Wall stretching for miles

Mutianyu

At 90km (55 miles) northeast of Beijing in Huairou County, Mutianyu is a little further from Beijing than Badaling, and thus less crowded. This granite-clad Ming-era bastion features several watchtowers and crenellated parapets. It is not actually a 'section' of the Great Wall, but an independent fortification guarding a particularly strategic entrance to Beijing. As at Badaling, the Ming restored this fortification based on a site originally fortified by the Northern Qi Dynasty that ruled the area in the 6th century AD.

While Mutianyu certainly has its share of souvenir shops, the atmosphere is much less frenetic than at Badaling. Another difference is that the foliage is much richer and, during the autumn, the turning leaves of the sycamore trees are a bright red. Reaching the nearest part of the wall is a good hour's walk and rather steep, but a cable car is available. The restored section of the wall is about 2km (1¼ miles) in length.

Open: 6.30am–6pm. Admission charge. Best transportation option is via Beijing Sightseeing Bus Centre near Tiananmen Square, tel: (010) 8353 1111.

Simatai

This section of the wall is 120km (75 miles) northeast of Beijing and has not been restored. Simatai offers an experience rather different from Badaling (some would say more authentic) and is popular with those who enjoy hiking. Although the cable car takes you from the car park to near the base of the wall, from here you walk unprotected along the 19km (11-mile) base of the wall, sometimes up rather narrow staircases – which locals call *tianti*, meaning a 'stairway to heaven'. The rewards for such endeavours are the views – a large watchtower called **Wanjing Lou (Viewing the Capital Tower)** affords one of the most spectacular views of the Great Wall available. Depending on your tastes, it's either exhilarating or terrifying. There is talk of restoring Simatai to make it more accessible to those with acrophobia.

Open: 8am–5pm. Admission charge. Best transportation option is via Beijing Sightseeing Bus Centre near Tiananmen Square, tel: (010) 8353 1111.

Jinshanling

About 15km (10 miles) to the west of Simatai is another section of the wall that attracts those seeking to escape the crowds. Many of the watchtowers have been restored. It is less precipitous than Simatai here, and so better suited to those who don't mind a hike, but don't like heights. This area, which lies in a broad valley, was particularly popular with Mongol raiders making their way to Beijing, and was one of the routes used by Kublai Khan when he invaded China. It is possible to follow the wall from here to the east to Simatai.

Open: 8am–5pm. Admission charge. Take a minibus from the Dongzhimen Long Distance Bus Station.

North of Beijing

This section covers a wide and disparate section of Northern China, admittedly bound only by the fact that the sights are geographically north of the capital and too far for a day trip from it. Included are parts of Hebei Province, which essentially surrounds the capital, and Liaoning, Jilin and Heilongjiang Provinces. From the cultural treasures of the Qing Dynasty Imperial Resort in Hebei, to the ice palaces of Harbin, there's a bit of everything here.

Formerly called Manchuria, this little-visited region covers a vast, mountainous and sparsely populated territory in the provinces of Liaoning, Jilin and Heilongjiang and is the ancestral homeland of China's last dynasty, the Qing. Historically, its nomads took any opportunity that Chinese weakness offered to cross the Great Wall and ravage the rich lands to the south. The last time this occurred was in 1644, when the Manchu ruler Shunzi seized control, establishing the Qing Dynasty on the 'throne of heaven' in Beijing.

The Manchus, a people of Tartar stock, were set on the road to glory by their ruler Nurhachi, who united the tribes and became khan in 1616, ruling from his palace at Shenyang. In the 20th century, Manchuria became a symbol of China's weakness: under Russian military control from 1900, it fell to the Japanese in 1932 and became the base for their puppet state of Manchukuo. The Northeast has much to offer visitors, but few infrastructural facilities to help them on the way. Warm in summer, the region is subject to viciously cold temperatures in winter.

Bordering Russia and North Korea, it is noted for its frigid winters but beautifully stark land- and seascapes. Changbai Shan (Ever-White Mountain) and Tian Chi (Heaven's Lake), on the border with North Korea, are a UNESCO Biosphere Reserve and China's largest nature reserve (*see pp122–3*). This area is the natural habitat of the endangered Siberian Tiger.

Beidaihe

The British surveyors who, in the late 19th century, discovered this pleasant spot on the seaside just south of Shanhaiguan informed their compatriots living in Tianjin and Beijing, who built seaside villas here. After 1949, these sumptuous residences were appropriated by the Communist Party for summer conferences. Now Beidaihe is visited by Beijing's middle classes who drive out for the weekend during the summer. Spring and autumn are a good time to visit, when the weather is not too cold and the beaches less crowded. The bicycles available for rent here are a good way to appreciate the ocean breezes outside the bustle of town.

Located 300km (186 miles) east of Beijing. Buses and trains can take you to the nearby town of Qinhuangdao from Beijing in about 3 hours. From there it's 20 minutes by taxi or bus to Beidaihe.

Changchun

The largely industrial capital of Jilin Province is known as a centre of automobile production but the car factories are in the suburbs and the city centre is actually quite attractive. Between 1932 and 1945 Changchun was the capital of the Japanese puppet state of Manchukuo, which the invaders used as a political fig leaf to veil their naked aggression towards China. It was here that the last Qing Dynasty emperor, Pu Yi, who had been forced to abdicate in

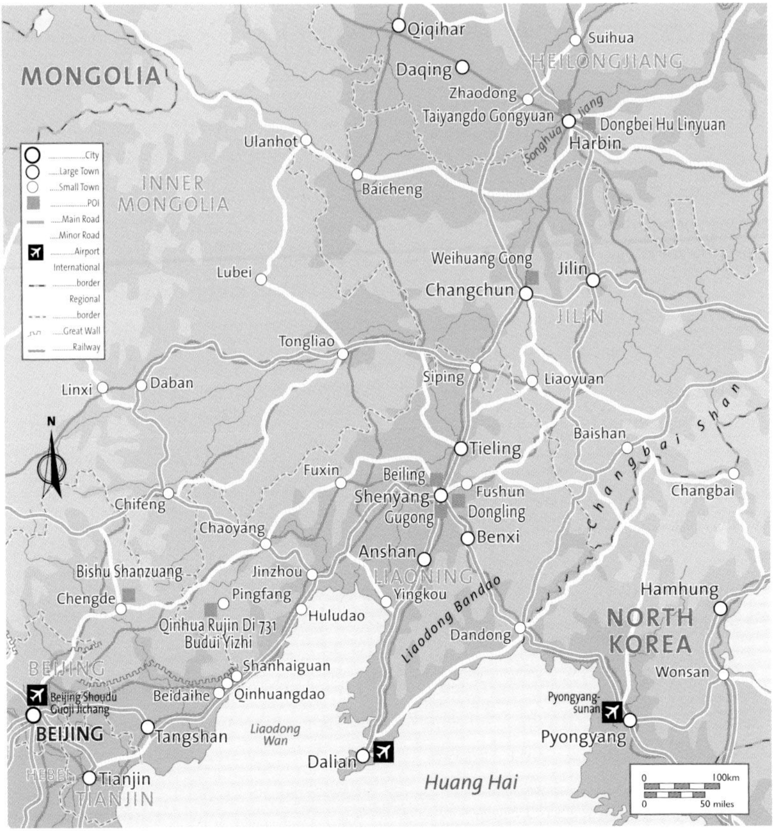

The Imperial Summer Resort near Chengde

1911, was reinstated as emperor, ruling over Manchukuo as a Japanese puppet, only to be taken captive by Soviet troops at the end of World War II. Returned to China, he was given a course of political re-education, then worked for seven years as a gardener in the Beijing Botanical Gardens before his death in 1967. (Bertolucci's *The Last Emperor* was a cinematic recreation of his tragicomic life.)
Changchun is 1½ hours from Beijing by air, 8 hours by bus, and around 10 hours by train.

Weihuang Gong (Palace Museum of the Last Emperor Pu Yi)
This palace served as the official residence of the last emperor during his 13-year reign as the so-called ruler of Japanese-occupied Manchuria, although Pu Yi often lived elsewhere. Quite a step down from the splendour of the Forbidden City, this is an attractive two-storey building of an anonymous but decidedly occidental style. The building has been meticulously restored and contains much memorabilia of Pu Yi, including his throne, bedchambers for himself and both his wives, and photographs of the emperor with his Japanese masters.
5 Guanfu Lu, Northeast Changchun. Open: 8.30am–5pm. Admission charge.

Chengde
In the hills of Hebei Province, northeast of Beijing, the Qing emperors established their **Bishu Shanzuang (Imperial Summer Resort)**. Far from the heat and clamour of the alien Han culture in Beijing, they felt more at home in this rugged area north of the Great Wall. This magnificent complex

of gardens, lakes, bridges, pagodas and palaces covers 5.6sq km (2sq miles) and is located in a river valley surrounded by mountains. The area has been classified as a UNESCO World Heritage Site.

Hunting, fishing and martial sports amused the Qing emperors when they resided here, but they also took time to meet with non-Han subjects of their empire, notably Mongols and Tibetans. To impress and welcome these guests, the Manchu Qing emperors constructed several temples outside the palace grounds which gave recognition to the religious faiths of the visitors, mainly the Lamaism embraced by the Tibetans and Mongols.

At the south end of the complex, just beyond the modern town of Chengde, lies the **Zheng Gong (Main Palace)** (*Open: 7am–5pm. Admission charge*) where the emperor resided and conducted affairs of state. The palace is now a museum. In addition to rare jade and porcelain pieces, it exhibits sedan chairs on which the emperors made the seven-day journey from Beijing with an entourage of thousands. Branching out from the Main Palace are separate buildings where the empress, as well as the concubines, resided. Behind the palace, gardens recreate scenes from Suzhou and other major Chinese cities and, further north, there are more pavilions where administrative and artistic tasks were performed by the emperor's immense staff of bureaucrats, eunuchs and artists.

Outside the walls of the palace lie the **Waiba Miao (eight outer temples)** constructed for visiting dignitaries from afar. These temples are much more than walking distance from the palace complex, and are usually visited by the minibus tours readily available from Chengde town, or by bicycle. The only active temple, and probably the most

(*continued on p78*)

Bicycle repair man in Chengde

Development vs the environment

All major industrial powers in history have achieved their success at the expense of the environment, placing development before environmental concerns. Britain, the USA and Japan all polluted their way to prosperity and began the clean-up only when the middle classes created by industrial development demanded clean air and water. Sometimes the efforts came too late – the London killer fog of December 1952, caused by coal smoke, remains the biggest single environmental disaster of modern times. China is following this ignoble path but with a significant difference – while the pace of economic development (and the attendant pollution) is unprecedented, large segments of the population still live in poverty. Add to this the worldwide concern over the global warming phenomena, and the problem is truly staggering in scope.

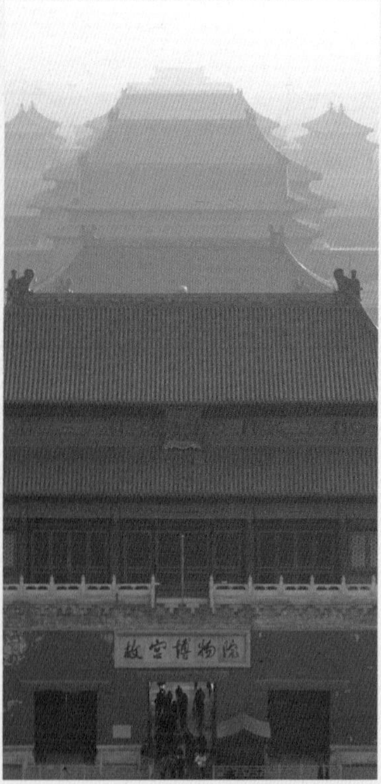

Pollution hangs over the Forbidden City

No visitor to China will be surprised to learn that 16 of the world's 20 most polluted cities are in China, or that only 1 per cent of the urban population breathes air considered safe by international standards. Water-borne pollution is just as serious, with major lakes now unfit even for agricultural irrigation and much of the sea coast red with algae, which kills all marine life. By most counts, China became the world's biggest polluter in 2007. The airborne pollution from China spreads not only over Asia, but as far away as the USA.

As in 1952 London, the culprit for air pollution is coal. China relies on its abundant coal supplies for its energy

Pollution over Beihai Lake, Beijing

needs and uses more coal than Europe, Japan and the USA combined. The heavy industries, such as steel and cement making, that have propelled growth, run exclusively on coal-fired power plants. Sadly, the country is choking on its own success.

China's government is painfully aware of the problems and is making efforts to change the practices that are polluting the country. The much maligned Three Gorges Dam is only one of many hydro-electric dams under construction. The 'development first' policies of the Deng era are being scaled back somewhat, as government-controlled prices for water and electricity are raised, but the authorities also fear 'social instability' (a polite way of saying a massive revolt against the Communist Party), which would result if the economy cooled dramatically and cost workers their jobs. On the other hand, there have been many instances of local protests by villagers outraged by polluting factories. There is truly no easy solution to the problem.

impressive, is **Puning Si** (*Open: 8am–5pm. Admission charge*), which was built in 1755 to commemorate Emperor Qianlong's victory over Mongol rebels. The complex is an interesting synthesis of Tibetan and Chinese architectural styles. In the central Mahayana Hall a 22m (73ft) tall wooden statue of the Buddhist Goddess of Mercy Guanyin takes pride of place. Tibetan elements are found in the stupas, or *chorten* in Tibetan, which hold sacred relics of the Buddha or the ashes of revered monks. Lamaist monks perform religious rites and chant in the temple.

The **Putouzongcheng Temple** (*Open: 8am–5pm. Admission charge*) is the largest of the eight outer temples and was built to resemble the Potala Palace in Lhasa. The temple is on a hillside with the Potala-like structures at the top. A pair of intricately carved sandalwood pagodas stand 19m (62ft) tall in one of the courtyards. The temple also houses an interesting collection of Tibetan religious artefacts, including the religious scrolls called *thankas* which vividly depict the Lamaist deities.

Other temples surrounding the Imperial Summer Resort worth seeing

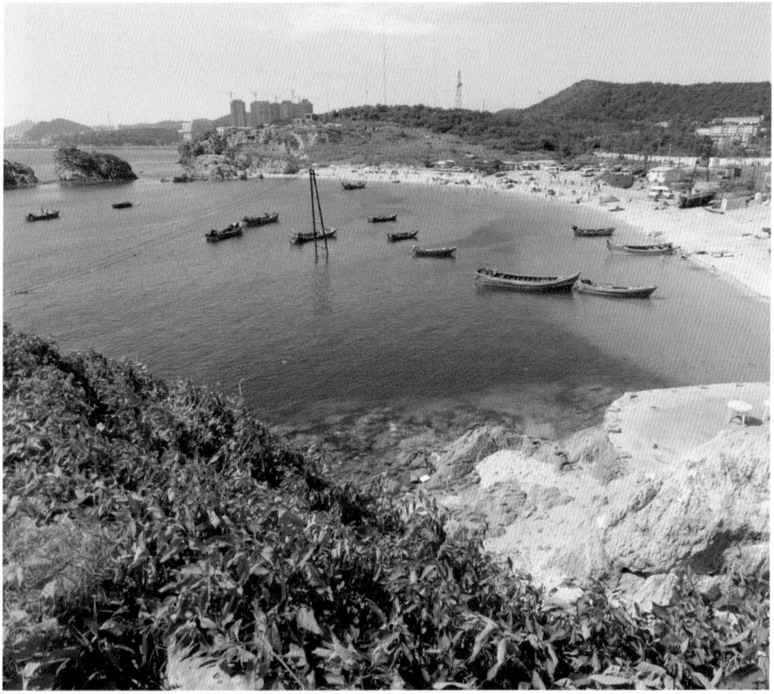

Fishermen's boats in a quiet cove off Laohutan Bay near Dalian

Dalian City as seen from one of its grassy parks

are **Pule Si**, which resembles the Temple of Heaven in Beijing, and **Xumifushou**, built to commemorate the visit of the Panchen Lama in 1781.

Chengde lies 250km (155 miles) northeast of Beijing. It can be reached by car in 2½ hours (slightly longer by bus), or in 4–5 hours by train.

Dalian

Dalian is a major port and a seaside resort situated on the southern tip of Liaodong Peninsula, which separates the Yellow Sea from the Liaodong Gulf. Dalian is considered by many to be the best-planned, attractive and liveable large city in the country, often compared favourably to Shanghai. The locals are proud of their city's ambience, and add to it with their pleasant but sophisticated demeanour. The city's harbour, once known as Port Arthur, was a Russian 'concession' until it was occupied by the Japanese. As a result of this, Dalian has a legacy of Tsarist and Japanese architecture to add to its scenic location. Its beaches are crowded in summer, but there is much rugged and open coastline nearby.

Dalian is not visited for its ancient sites but for its attractive modern metropolitan atmosphere, good weather and lovely coastline. Within the city, the central Zhongshan Guangchang (Zhongshan Square) is surrounded by colonial buildings from the Russian era and large open spaces of grassy parks. Nearby Tianjin Jie is a pedestrianised street good for shopping. The **Xiandi Bowuguan (Dalian Modern Museum)** (*10 Huizhan. Tel: (0411) 8480 1052. Open: 9am–5pm. Admission charge*) has some modern art and gives a nod to the city's history but looks more towards the future.

The best parts of Dalian lie along the coast. Closest to town, at about

ETHNIC MINORITIES OF THE NORTHEAST

China officially recognises 55 minority 'nationalities' in addition to the Han majority. Minorities comprise about 9 per cent of the country's population. The largest minority living in Northern China are the Manchus (10 million), descendants of the race who ruled China's last dynasty, the Qing. The Manchus are totally integrated into modern society, but along the border regions of Heilongjiang Province three fascinating groups of distinct ethnicity – the Oroqen, Ewenki and the Hezhen peoples – still pursue traditional lifestyles, hold shamanistic beliefs and speak their own languages. The Oroqen are known as skilled hunters. The Ewenki use reindeer for transport and live in birch bark and hide tents. The Hezhen traditionally make all their clothing from fish skins. Needless to say, these traditional lifestyles are disappearing as the lure of the city life entices the youths.

4km (2½ miles) distant is **Donghai Gongyuan (Donghai Park)** (*Open: 8am–5pm. Admission charge*) and, a bit further south, **Bangchuidao Jingqu (Bangchuidao Scenic Area)** (*Open: 8am–5pm. Admission charge*). Both can be reached by taxi in ten minutes. Continuing along the coast, there are two ocean-themed amusement parks with dolphin shows and aquariums, **Laohutan Leyuan (Tiger Beach Ocean Park)** and **Shengya Haiyang Shijie (Sun Asia Ocean World)** (*Tel: (0411) 8458 1113. Open: daily. Admission charge*). Both can be reached by taxi in about 20 minutes.

Dalian has an international airport, with international flights to Japan and Korea. A flight to Beijing takes an hour; by train it is 12 hours.

Harbin

Situated on the banks of the Songhua River, the capital of Heilongjiang Province is an industrial centre and railway junction. In January and February, the citizens take advantage of Harbin's (sometimes spelt Haerbin, and

Turkic Muslims at a market in Xinjiang

correctly pronounced with three syllables) sub-zero temperatures to hold their world-renowned, spectacular Bingdeng Jie (Ice Lantern Festival). The city has a strong Russian influence, which began when the Russians constructed a railway line in the late 19th century from Vladivostok to Dalian, passing through Harbin. White Russian émigrés arrived after the Bolshevik revolution in 1917, and refugees, largely Jewish, arrived during World War II. In the Daoliqu district, Russian architecture abounds where trees line cobbled streets, especially along the Zhongyang Dajie pedestrianised street.

Dongbei Hu Linyuan (Siberian Tiger Park)
Outside of Harbin, this park, while interesting, can be distressing for some visitors. A captive breeding centre for the endangered Siberian Tiger, the centre has achieved its goal – over 300 cubs have been born here – but the animals are not kept in good conditions. The coup de grâce is the feeding of live poultry and calves to the tigers, which seems to delight Chinese tourists.
15km (9 miles) north of Sun Island Park, Harbin. Tel: (0451) 8819 1181. Open: 8.30am–6pm. Admission charge.

Sheng Suofeiya Jiaotang (St Sophia Cathedral)
The splendid Byzantine-style domed Russian Orthodox cathedral matches the northern atmosphere here, although it now serves as an architectural museum showing interesting photographs of Russian life in old Harbin.
Corner of Toulong and Diduan. Open: 8.30am–5pm. Admission charge.

Taiyangdao Gongyuan (Sun Island Park)
On the opposite bank of the Songhua River from the unpromisingly named (and unimaginatively conceived) Sidalin Gongyuan (Stalin Park), the Sun Island Park is being developed as a summer and winter outdoor leisure centre. Extending to almost 4,000ha (9,884 acres), it has a lake, parks, ornamental gardens and forests. This is one of the sites where the Ice Lantern Festival takes place in January.
North bank of the Songhua River. Open: 8.30am–4.30pm. Admission charge.

Pingfang

Qinhua Rijiun Di 731 Budui Yizhi (Japanese Germ Warfare Experimental Base)
Also known as Unit 731, during World War II this is where both Chinese and foreign prisoners of war (whom the Japanese referred to as 'logs') were subjected to experiments that reached the edge of human barbarity. The exhibition is largely photographical, but it's not for the faint of heart.

Pingfang village. Tel: (0451) 8680 1556. Open: 9.00–11.30am, 1–5pm. Admission charge.

Shanhaiguan

In Hebei Province, some 350km (220 miles) east of Beijing, the Great Wall reaches the sea. It was here that the Manchu warriors who established the Qing Dynasty entered China proper. Relying on a mixture of guile and bribery, they fought no battle but were simply allowed to pass.

In 2006, a massive restoration project was undertaken on this old walled town, levelling and then rebuilding the old Ming-era buildings. While the result is attractive, the atmosphere is decidedly commercial. Several sections of the Great Wall have also been restored here. The First Pass under Heaven, east of town, has an impressive gatehouse, and north of town at Jiao Shan the wall reaches the sea. Good hiking opportunities abound here, but there is a cable car as well.

Buses and trains can take you to the nearby town of Qinhuangdao from Beijing in about 3 hours. From there it's 20 minutes by taxi or bus to Shanhaiguan to the north or Beidailhe to the south.

Shenyang

Capital of Liaoning Province, Shenyang is an industrial city and a base for travellers wanting to get off the beaten track and explore parts of old Manchuria. It was the Manchus' capital from 1625 until they took Beijing in 1644 and established the Qing Dynasty.

Shenyang lies 700km (438 miles) northeast of Beijing. It can be reached by air in 1 hour, or in 8 to 10 hours by train or bus.

Posters of legendary warriors stand guard on a door in Shenyang

Beiling (North Tomb)
Located in the Beiling Park in the northern suburbs of the city, the spectacular tomb of Abahai, son of the Manchu Emperor Nurhachi, was completed in 1651 but has later Qing Dynasty additions. The 'sacred way', lined with animals carved in stone, is reminiscent of the more impressive imperial tombs around Beijing.
12 Taishan Lu, North Shenyang. Tel: (024) 8689 6294. Open: 6am–7pm (summer); 8am–5pm (winter). Admission charge.

Dongling (East Tomb)
This is the tomb of the Manchu ruler Nurhachi, grandfather of Shunzhi, the first Qing Dynasty emperor. Situated outside Shenyang, it encapsulates in miniature the style that the Qing emperors would later perfect in Beijing.
Located in a forest park about 8km (5 miles) east of Shenyang. Open: 9am–4pm (summer); 10am–3pm (winter). Admission charge.

Gugong (Imperial Palace)
Built in 1625–36 during the reigns of the pre-Qing Dynasty rulers Nurhachi and Abahai, the palace remained the Manchu seat until their transfer to the Forbidden City in Beijing. Manchu architectural norms dominate Chinese ones in the complex, and the palace is small enough to get around easily yet big enough to give a feeling of the Qing rulers' driving ambition. Among the

Roofscape of the Dragon Throne, Imperial Palace, Shenyang

most important structures are the **Dazhen Dian (Hall of Great Affairs)**, the **Shiwang Ting (Pavilion of Ten Princes)** and the emperors' private apartments at the **Qingning Gong (Palace of Pure Tranquillity)**.
In the old city. Tel: (024) 2484 2215. Open: 9am–4pm (summer); 10am–3pm (winter). Admission charge.

Mao statue
Once a fixture in every Chinese city, gigantic statues of Mao now survive only in the peripheries of the country, so if you want to see one of these relics of China's past, in bronze at that, here's your chance.
Zhongshan Guangchang, central Shenyang.

South of Beijing

This chapter covers three provinces: Shanxi, Henan and Shandong. Shanxi, with its mountainous terrain and strategic location, has seen many centuries of turmoil and is one of China's earliest centres of Buddhism. Henan Province's Kaifeng and Luoyang served as capitals of ancient Chinese dynasties and with almost 100 million inhabitants this is China's most populous province. Shandong produced China's most famous son and one of the most influential persons to ever live, Confucius.

SHANXI PROVINCE

Shanxi offers fascinating Buddhist relics near the city of Datong, including the Buddhist sacred mountain of Wutai Shan and the Qing Dynasty banking capital of China, Pingyao, which is now a living museum of traditional architecture.

Datong

Just south of the Mongolian Plateau, this city is often described as 'grimy', which is neither unfair nor surprising since the city is surrounded by some of China's largest coal fields. Most people come to Datong to visit the Yungang Caves, but within this ancient walled city there are a few attractions that merit a visit. Datong was twice the capital of regional Chinese dynasties, first the Northern Wei (AD 386–494) and later the Liao (AD 907–1125), and sights from both these dynasties still survive in Datong city. In **Huayan Si (Huayan Monastery)** (*Huayan Si Jie. Open: 8am–5pm. Admission charge*), the Mahavira Hall is one of the largest temple buildings in China and houses 31 statues of the Buddha and his various incarnations. The five large gilded statues date from the Ming era. Just to the east lies **Jiulongbi (Nine Dragons Screen)**, a 45m (150ft) long intricately tiled 'spirit wall' built to give celestial protection according to principles of *feng shui* to the palace of a Ming prince who resided here. Apparently the calculations were off, since the palace itself burned down, but the wall remains.

Xuankong Si (Hanging Temple)

Further afield from Datong lies one of five mountains sacred to Daoists – Heng Shan. This 2,017m (6,620ft) peak is scaled by both the faithful (legend recounts that Qin Shi Huang, the man who united China, scaled the peak) and now more secular mountain climbers. The three-hour drive from Datong passes by loess landscapes and picturesque villages, but most people who travel here come to see the spectacular Hanging

Temple. Built into the side of a cliff 1,400 years ago, and augmented over the centuries, the Hanging Temple is a series of wooden pavilions built over the entrances of caves. The multi-storeyed pavilions are supported by posts and connected by walkways. Inside the caves, the stone has been carved into representations of religious objects from both Buddhism and Daoism.
65km (40 miles) southeast of Datong. Tel: (0352) 832 7417. Open: 7am–6pm. Admission charge. Minibus from Datong.

Yungang Shiku (Yungang Caves)
Located in the hills 16km (10 miles) east of Datong, the Yungang Cave temples are some of the earliest examples of Buddhist religious art in China. They were carved into the sandstone cliffs and hillsides over a period of 30 years by an army of some 40,000 workers during the Northern Wei Dynasty. Sometime after completing their magnificent monuments, the Wei decamped south to Luoyang and continued their stone

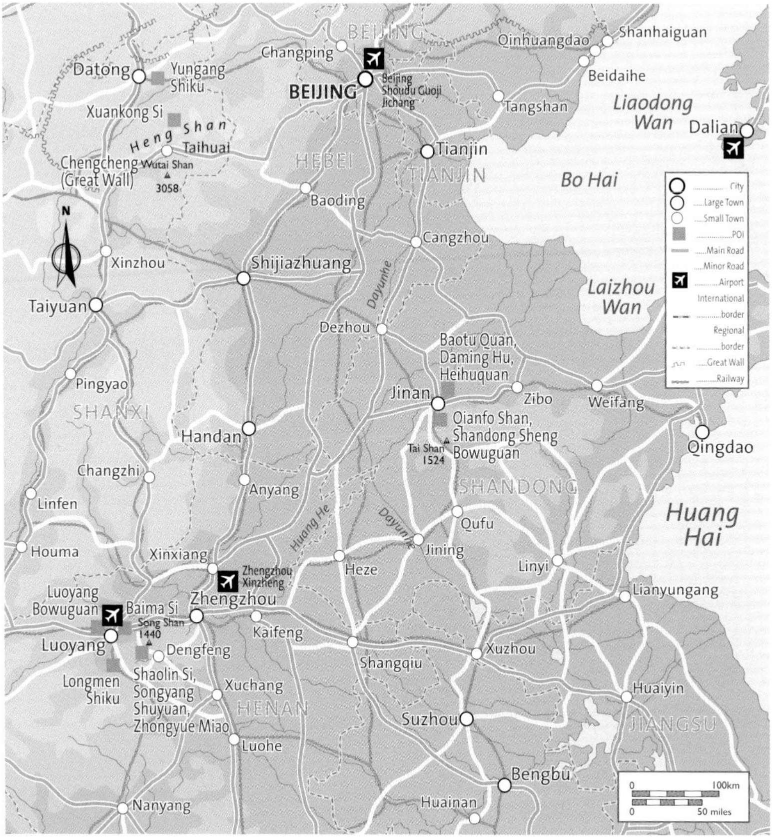

carving at Longmen. The elaborate statuary here ranges in size from minuscule to huge and, unlike later Buddhist religious art, has strong non-Chinese influences; Persian and even Hellenistic elements are visible. The only other comparable examples of this ancient Buddhist art in China are at another Northern Wei Dynasty site at Dunhuang, an oasis in distant Gansu Province.

Yungang has always been, and continues to be today, a pilgrimage site for devout Buddhists. Isolated and relatively unknown, the caves escaped early pillagers, unlike the Imperial Tombs and other sites closer to Beijing.

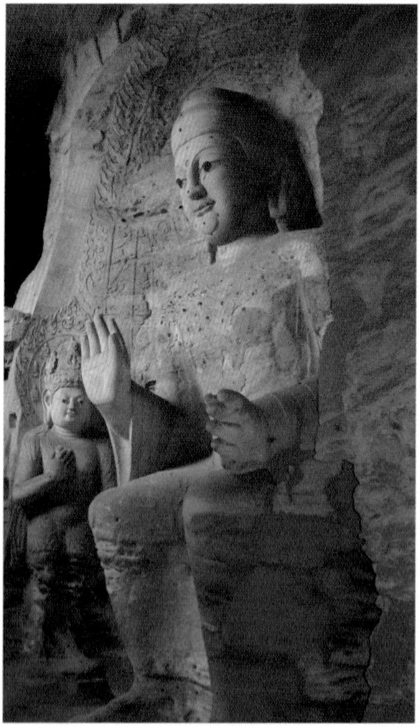
A stone Buddha in the Yungang Caves

It was only in the early 20th century, when the site was discovered by Westerners, that the legal looting began. Many of the smaller pieces were carted off by archaeologists 'for further study' and are now in museums and private collections in foreign countries. Still, there has been no indigenous depredation – the Red Guards never made it here.

The 53 caves vary greatly in size, contents and style. Some are not particularly deep, and contain a single huge standing Buddha image carved into the rear wall (Cave 5) and others (notably Cave 6) are elaborate temples, with Buddhist parables called *jataka* depicted in bas relief along the walls, ceilings and even carved into elaborate columns. One cave (Cave 8) even features carved images of the Hindu gods Vishnu and Shiva.

Tel: (0352) 510 2265. Open: 8.30am–5pm. Admission charge. Minibus from Datong.

Pingyao

This walled city was once the financial capital of China – today it has no bank and, going further against the trend, no cars. Established during the Ming Dynasty, it housed the first bank to issue cheques, payable at over 100 branches through China. A Pingyao bank was the official banker of the late Qing Dynasty, and when the dynasty fell, the banks collapsed with them. The town fell into penury and, with no natural advantages or resources and without funds to

Huayan Monastery, Datong

develop, Pingyao was largely forgotten. Something of the entrepreneurial spirit must have remained, for the city has since capitalised on its time-capsule atmosphere and is now a major tourist destination. The main street of the town, Nandao Jie, is full of souvenir shops, and tour groups are not uncommon.

The 8km (5-mile) restored city walls are 12m (39ft) high and punctuated by 72 watchtowers. Walking along them, you look down onto cobblestoned streets and courtyard houses that appear to have escaped the modernity all too prevalent in China today. Children frolic, oldsters stroll and caged birds chirp. One of the few specific sights in Pingyao is the **Rishengchang Financial House Museum**, one of the first banks to have been established in Pingyao. The museum's displays are interesting, but it's the sprawling architecture that captures the visitor. The Bell Tower near the North Gate offers fine views. The bankers were fairly secular – there are no significant religious sights in Pingyao. Two attractive and relaxed temples are within easy cycling distance, leaving Pingyao from the south.

About 100km (60 miles) south of Taiyuan. Admission charge for entering the town covers all sights such as the city walls and museum. 2 hours by bus or train from Taiyuan.

Taihuai

The village of Taihuai lies in a valley surrounded by the five peaks of **Wutai Shan (Five Terrace Mountain)** (*see pp90–91*), and is a starting point for

(*continued on p90*)

Rural life

Since the unification of China under the 'First Emperor', Qin Shi Huang, in 221 BC, as indeed under a plethora of lesser states for millennia beforehand, the Chinese economy has rested on the hard labour of the great masses of its rural peasantry. Their lot has never been an easy one. Subject to the vicissitudes of the weather and the whims of a fickle court, they have suffered through the centuries from drought and famine, broken river banks and devastating floods, corrupt officials and arbitrarily fixed prices – not to mention annual forced labour without pay.

All this was meant to change after the Communist seizure of power in 1949. Mao Zedong's greatest intellectual contribution to the international Marxist movement was his inclusion of the peasantry in the revolutionary pantheon based on workers, intellectuals and soldiers. Indeed, Mao placed the peasant at the head of this revolutionary force, standing Marx and Lenin on their heads by promoting the concept of agrarian revolution before that of an industrialised revolution carried out by the urban proletariat.

Planting rice can be back-breaking work

In the event, Mao's vision did not work at all well. Land reforms were carried out, and initially this was well received by the peasantry. After 1949, a massive programme of land reform was implemented nationwide, dispossessing and often killing landlords, and redistributing land to the peasants who tilled it. This seems to have been popular with the rural poor, but Mao was determined to go further. First, rural families were reorganised into cooperatives, with land held not by the poor peasantry, but collectively by the state. Next, land was collectivised, combining several cooperatives. Finally, 'people's communes' were established, with all land belonging to the state, while even farming implements were held collectively as all private property was

Transporting ducks and geese to the local market

banished. This was not at all popular with the poor peasants in whose name the Communist revolution had been carried out, and many rural farmers slaughtered their livestock rather than turn it over to the state.

Meanwhile, most of the Communist government's energies and resources were not put into the agricultural sector, but into industry, with the emphasis on heavy industrialisation and the goal of overtaking middle-ranking capitalist countries like the United Kingdom in 'ten or twenty years'. At best, agricultural production more or less kept pace with the expanding population, while at times of political experimentation – like the 'Great Leap Forward' in 1958–60, agricultural production fell disastrously, leading to widespread starvation and the death of between 20 and 40 million people, most of them poor peasants.

This catastrophic experiment was compounded in 1966–76 by the wild excesses of the Great Proletarian Cultural Revolution, when intellectuals were persecuted; education ground to a halt, and both agricultural and industrial production fell drastically. It is now widely estimated that 36 million people were persecuted in rural China alone, while as many as 1.5 million died.

By 1976, following the death of Mao Zedong, people had had enough – and not just the hard-pressed peasantry, but party officials too. Under Deng Xiaoping and his successors policies were reversed, the commune system scrapped, and land redistributed to the peasantry. Economic reforms, including the gradual introduction of a free market economy and incentives based on private initiative, were introduced.

Today, the lot of the Chinese peasant remains hard – but it is still probably better than it has ever been before in Chinese history. Nearly six decades after Mao proclaimed the People's Republic in the name of the workers, peasants and soldiers, China's vast rural population can at last aspire to increasing freedom, security and wealth.

Pingyao city walls

visits to the temples on the mountainsides. The village itself is filled with temples, notably the Tibetan-style **Tayuan Temple** with its characteristic white *dagoba* (the Tibetan word for the Buddhist reliquary shrine also known as a 'pagoda' or 'stupa'). The **Luohou Temple**, dating from the Ming Dynasty, houses a beautifully enamelled and gilded lotus flower, with each of its eight petals covering a seated Buddha image. As the lotus rotates, the images are individually revealed. On the outskirts of Taihuai, the **Bronze Temple**, made entirely from this metal, glows like burnished gold and houses a vast collection of intricate Buddha images.

Each of the five terraces, named after the cardinal points of the compass plus a 'central' terrace, has its own temple. The **Bodhisattva Peak** is reached by a climb of 108 steps – the number of beads used in Buddhist prayer beads. To the east lies **Dailuo Peak**, which offers great views of Taihuai and the surrounding peaks and can be reached by cable car. The **Nanshan Temple** to the south is less visited and has significant Taoist elements in its architecture and decorations, such as statues of the faith's Eight Immortals. Wutai Shan and particularly Taihuai are very crowded in the summer months. Since good Buddhists rise early, the usual plan of doing so to beat the crowds is fruitless – better to visit the sights in the late afternoon. Too many temples can be mind-boggling, so take advantage of the area's natural beauty as well.

About 240km (150 miles) southeast of Datong – about a 4-hour bus ride, or less by private car. Open: all temples open early–5pm. Admission charge for each temple.

Wutai Shan (Five Terrace Mountain)

Travelling further south in Shanxi Province, you reach Wutai Shan, the

northernmost of China's four sacred Buddhist mountains. The name means 'Five Terrace Mountain' referring to the various peaks, the highest of which reaches 3,058m (10,033ft). This area has been a centre of Buddhist veneration since the faith reached China, and is believed to be the home on earth of the bodhisattva Manjusri, one of the Buddha's disciples. As Guanyin is the goddess of Mercy, Manjusri represents the virtue of wisdom. She is depicted in many statues as carrying a sword – used to cut away ignorance. Many of the temples of Wutai Shan are dedicated to her memory.
About 2km (1¼ miles) from the village of Taihuai.

HENAN PROVINCE

Baima Si (White Horse Temple)

The Buddhist temple founded here in AD 68 was the first in China. It has been rebuilt numerous times since the days when two monks arrived from India on white horses, bringing with them the sutras (ancient religious and philosophical texts) which they translated into Chinese. All the temple structures are recreations, mostly from the Ming era, and they include the hall where the original sutras are kept in a drawer.

The gateways are flanked by statues of the horses that carried the monks from India, while the monks themselves are buried in the walls.
10km (6 miles) east of Luoyang. Open: 8am–6pm. Admission charge.

Huang He (Yellow River)

China's second longest river, the Huang He, rises in the Bayar Shan mountains of Qinghai and flows through Inner Mongolia before snaking across Northern Central China, covering a total of 4,630km (2,877 miles) on its journey to the Bo Hai Gulf, southeast of Tianjin. Some of China's earliest settlements, dating back to 6,000 BC, arose in the fertile plain created by the river. It was once known as 'China's Sorrow' because of its tendency to produce drastic floods. In 1642, a flood took 300,000 lives, in 1887, 500,000 died, but the most deplorable flooding occurred in June 1938 when Chiang Kai Shek, fleeing Japanese forces, ordered

The White Horse Temple

Boats on the Yellow River

the Yellow River dykes dynamited. The Japanese sidestepped the floods, but the Generalissimo Chiang Kai Shek killed an estimated 400,000 of his own people. The river's negative impact has been reduced by dykes and other control measures. There are a number of interesting towns along its banks.

Kaifeng

This charming walled city located 9km (6 miles) south of the Yellow River has been the capital of seven Chinese dynasties. It reached its historical apogee during the Northern Song Dynasty (AD 960–1126) when it had a population of well over a million. It then contained palaces, temples and libraries, making it one of the largest and most cultured cities in the world. The floodwaters of the Yellow River swept this and later incarnations of the city away – most of what you see today dates from the Ming and Qing periods. Greater Kaifeng now has a population of over 5 million, but the major sights of interest are within the city walls. Kaifeng is famous as the home of China's Jewish community, who settled here in the 10th century after arriving from Persia via the Silk Road.

The nearest airport to Kaifeng is at Zhengzhou, 70 km (43½ miles) to the west. Buses arrive from Zhengzhou or Luoyang.

Da Xiangguo Si (Prime Minister's Temple)

In the centre of the walled city, this was China's largest Buddhist temple during

the Song Dynasty with thousands of monks chanting the sutras in 64 halls. The temple was destroyed by floods in 1642 and rebuilt in 1766. An octagonal pavilion within the complex holds the primary artistic attraction here, a four-sided statue of Guanyin, the Buddhist Goddess of Mercy. The statue was carved from a single gingko tree and is now covered with gold leaf. The statue's 1,000 arms and eyes symbolise the all-seeing and all-compassionate nature of the deity.
54 Ziyou. Tel: (0378) 566 5090.
Open: 8am–6pm. Admission charge.

Shanshaangan Huiguan (Shanshaangan Guild Hall)
Lying just to the north of the Prime Minister's Temple, this vibrant Qing-era structure was once the home, offices and ceremonial centre of visiting merchants from the three provinces of Shanxi, Shaanxi and Gansu. In addition to a spirit wall and drum and bell tower, the interesting features to note are the intricate painting and carvings on both the wood and stone surfaces of the main hall.
Xufu. Tel: (0378) 595 7411.
Open: 8am–6pm. Admission charge.

Longmen Shiku (Longmen Caves)
Undoubtedly the most spectacular sights in the vicinity of Luoyang are the Buddhist cave carvings at Longmen. In this vast 'sculpture park' of 1,352 grottoes there are more than 100,000 Buddha images, ranging in height from a few centimetres to 18m (59ft). Built

Chinese gardens in Kaifeng

The Dragon Gate Cave of Longmen

over a period of 600 years, the earliest date from AD 494, when they were begun under the orders of the Northern Wei Dynasty emperor Xiao Wen, who had recently moved the Wei capital from Datong to Luoyang. These earliest statues are in the **Binyang Dong (Binyang Caves)**, the first you reach upon entering the area. Like their predecessors at Yungang, the caves have interesting non-Chinese elements in the Buddhist motifs since the faith had only recently arrived in China from India via Persia.

Further along, both on foot and in time, lies **Wanfo Dong (Ten Thousand Buddha Cave)**, which was created during the late 7th-century Tang Dynasty. The Tang Empress Wu Zetian was an ardent supporter of Buddhism, and believed herself to be an incarnation of Guanyin, the Buddhist Goddess of Mercy. She thus commissioned **Fengxian Si (Ancestor Worshipping Cave)**, the most impressive sight at Longmen, with the face of the central figure carved to resemble the empress.

Sadly, these artistic and religious masterpieces have fallen victim to various depredations over time. Many smaller statues have been carted off by unscrupulous collectors, while the faces of those too large to steal have been gouged away by various fanatics. If time permits, take a boat across the Yi River to the village of Dongshan. There are more caves here, but the trip is made truly worthwhile by the

perspective it offers of the Longmen caves in their entirety.
Located 14km (8½ miles) south of Luoyang, along the Yi River, stretching for about 1km (⅔ mile). Tel: (0379) 595 7645. Open: 6.30am–7pm. Admission charge.

Luoyang

This city of 1 million inhabitants lies 30km (18½ miles) south of the Yellow River in Henan Province. Founded around 1200 BC, it was intermittently the capital of China from the Eastern Zhou Dynasty (770 BC) until the Later Tang (AD 936). It is sometimes considered the eastern terminus of the Silk Route, and is home to the first Buddhist temple in China.
Luoyang has an airport with connections to Beijing and Xian. It is also on the rail line from Shanghai to Xian. A bus service connects it with destinations to the north, such as Datong, and to the east, along the Yellow River Valley.

Luoyang Bowuguan (Luoyang Municipal Museum)

The museum contains many relics from Luoyang's days of glory, including maps of the city and artefacts recovered from tombs such as sculpted horses.
Zhongzhou. Adjacent to Wangcheng Gongyuan (Wangcheng Park). Tel: (0379) 393 7107. Open: 8.30am–5.30pm. Admission charge.

SONG SHAN SCENIC AREA

Song Shan is the name given to three mountain peaks sacred to the Taoist

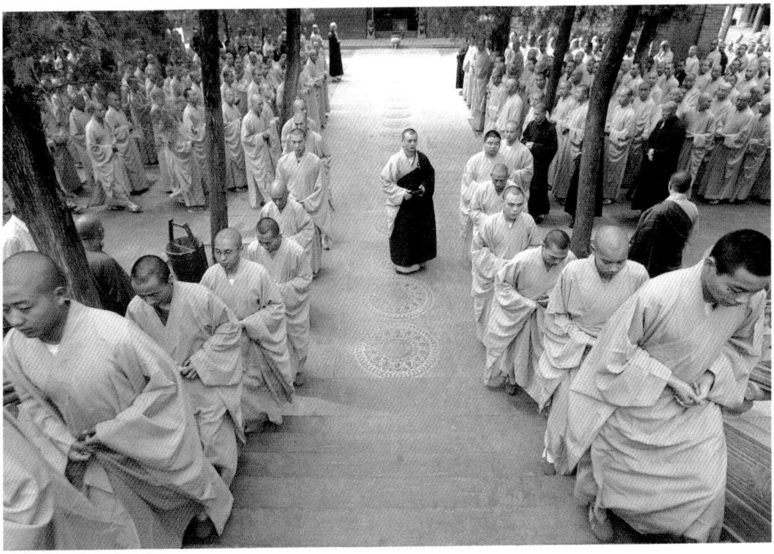

Monks celebrating the Buddha's birth at Shaolin Temple

The Forest of Pagodas in Shaolin Temple

faith, but Buddhist and Confucian sites are also found here. The mountains are located in Henan Province, south of the Yellow River, about halfway between Luoyang and Zhengzhou. The various sights on the mountains are best accessed from the town of Dengfeng, located to the south. While there are several interesting sights, the best known is the **Shaolin Si (Shaolin Temple)** home of the 'fighting monks'. It has a venerable history dating back to AD 495, but the temple is now a victim of its own success, largely due to the film exploits of Bruce Lee and his Western imitators, and more of a tourist attraction than a monastery or martial arts centre.

Shaolin Si (Shaolin Temple)

With the large number of visitors it is hard to believe that there are really any serious resident monks here, although charlatans offering 'secret techniques' are in abundance. Still, there are some interesting sights at Shaolin, such as the Wenshi Hall, the Pilu Pavilion and Chuipu Hall, which has large ceramic figures depicting the fighting stances. The **Shaolin Talin (Forest of Pagodas)**, outside the main temple area, provides respite from the crowds, and a 3km (2-mile) walk through the forest leads to Damo Cave where a famous monk is said to have meditated for nine years.

Located 15km (9 miles) west of Dengfeng. Tel: (0371) 274 9204. Open: 8am–5pm. Admission charge.

Songyang Shuyuan (Songyang Academy)

A kilometre (2/3 mile) or so outside Dengfeng, this is a Confucian centre of

study that reached its peak of popularity during the Tang Dynasty. Two cypress trees said to be over 4,000 years old were given the rank of general by a Han Dynasty emperor who visited here.
Open: 8am–5pm.
Admission charge.

Zhongyue Miao (Zhongyue Temple)

Less frenetic than Shaolin, this is an active Taoist temple with elaborate statuary and frescoes of the Taoist pantheon. It has 11 main buildings and covers 100 sq km (62 sq miles).
4km (2½ miles) east of Dengfeng.
Open: 6.30am–6.30pm.
Admission charge.

SHANDONG PROVINCE

Shandong Province is famous for Jinan, the attractive provincial capital on the Yellow River, Qufu, the home town of the sage Confucius, and the German architecture (and beer) of Qingdao.

Jinan

Renowned as the City of Springs, the capital of Shandong Province was founded in the 8th century BC and flourished as a commercial centre during the Tang Dynasty (AD 618–907). Its springs are not as impressive as they used to be, as a result of lower water levels in the underground aquifers.
15km (9 miles) from the south bank of the Yellow River on the Beijing–Shanghai railway line.

Song Shan Scenic Area

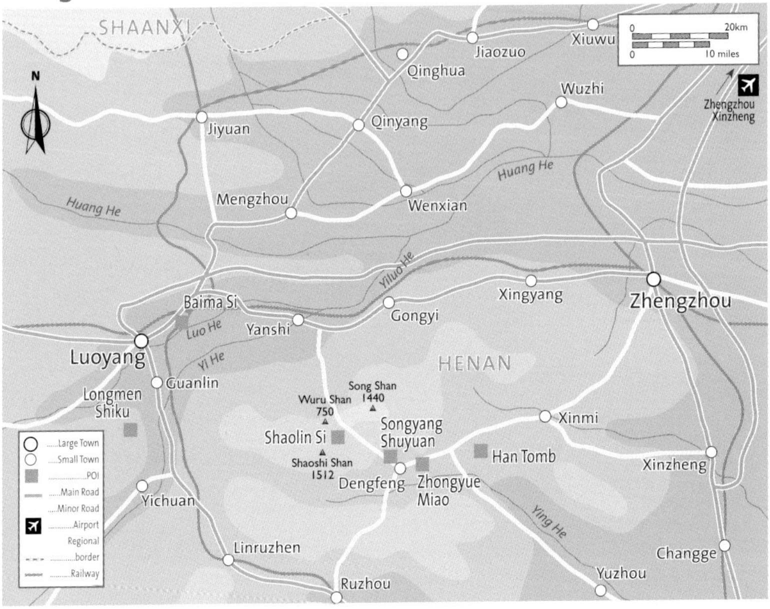

Baotu Quan (Jet Spring)
Also translated as the 'Gushing from the Ground Spring', Baotu Quan's waters emerge in a pond by means of three fountains in the gardens in which the spring is set. This spring is framed by pavilions, including the Song Dynasty Luoyuan Tang (Source of the Luo Hall) and the Guanlian Ting (Wave-Viewing Pavilion).
Baotu Quan. Next to the city moat. Open: 8am–5pm. Admission charge.

Daminghu (Daming Lake)
Weeping willows, gardens, playgrounds, teahouses and pavilions adorn the banks of the 'Lake of Great Brightness', which suffers from the same lowered water table that affects Jinan's springs. Nevertheless, this is a welcome stretch of greenery and cool water in the heart of the city.
Daminghu. South of the Jinan–Qingdao railway line. Open: 8am–8pm. Admission charge.

Heihuquan (Black Tiger Spring)
The water originates in a cave at this park, and surges out of the mouths of three stone tigers in an area where many other springs emerge.
Heihuquan. East of the city centre. Open: 8am–5pm. Admission charge.

Bridge in Nanjiao Gardens in Jinan

Tricycle on the beach at Qingdao

Qianfo Shan (Thousand Buddha Mountain)

Buddhist images are carved into the cliffside here. At the top of a steep climb is the **Xingguo Si (Temple of the Flourishing State)**, with about 60 Buddha images ranging in height from 20cm (8in) to more than 3m (10ft), dating from the 6th century AD.

Qianfo Shan in the southern suburbs of Jinan. Tel: (0531) 691 1792. Open: 7am–6pm. Admission charge.

Shandong Sheng Bowuguan (Shandong Provincial Museum)

Moved from its former city-centre site, this museum still features an extensive collection of archaeological finds including frescoes, Buddhist sculptures, musical instruments and tomb ornaments. The most important single exhibit is a 4,000-year-old collection of Longshan black pottery. A 2,000-year-old treatise on the art of war, written on bamboo strips, is also on display.

Adjacent to Qianfo Shan (Thousand Buddha Mountain). Tel: (0531) 296 7179. Open: Tue–Sun 9am–5pm. Closed: Mon. Admission charge.

CHINA & TEA

Lu Yu, a Tang Dynasty Master of Tea, wrote that drinking tea aids the digestion, especially 'when sipped in the company of sweet and beautiful maidens in a pavilion by a water-lily pond or near a lacquered bridge'. Most tea drinkers will not be so fortunate, but as long as the tea is good, they may be willing to make allowances.

In the Chinese tea ceremony, the miniature cups and teapot are doused with scalding hot water; tea is then placed in the pot, and boiling water added. After a brief infusion, the pot is emptied into the cups and the infusing process repeated.

There are many varieties of Chinese tea, and although jasmine tea is usually served as a matter of course in restaurants, you could ask for black, green, oolong or herbal tea instead.

Dacheng Hall in Qufu

Qingdao

The town of Qingdao is located on the Yellow Sea at the tip of the Shandong Peninsula, 320km (200 miles) east of the provincial capital of Jinan. Its attractive seaside location is augmented by its fascinating German architecture. The Germans seized the area and were granted a 99-year lease from the tottering Qing Dynasty after two German missionaries were killed here during the Boxer Rebellion in 1897. German occupation lasted only until 1922 when, as a consequence of the Versailles Treaty, all German territories in Asia were transferred to Japan. In 1922 the Japanese left but returned from 1938 until the end of World War II.

The main beaches of Qingdao will probably disappoint those expecting fine sand and azure waters, but the coastal atmosphere is refreshing and the seafood restaurants are excellent. The real attraction of Qingdao is the German architecture and the atmosphere of the tree-lined cobbled streets of the hilly old town. The palace of the former governor, two churches (one Catholic, one Protestant), and the shops and villas in a mixture of Teutonic and Bavarian styles are unique in China.

Qingdao has also achieved worldwide fame for its beer (spelt Tsingtao on the bottles), brewed here using spring waters from the nearby Laoshan Mountain. While huge demand has meant moving the brewery outside town, the original German brewery is now an interesting museum called the **World of Tsingtao** (*58 Dengzhou. Tel: (0532) 8383 3437. Open: 9am–4pm*). The Qingdao International Beer Festival is held during the last two weeks of August and attracts over a million visitors.

Qufu

Qufu is an attractive small town and an emblematic spot as the birthplace of Confucius (Kong Fuzi), the most influential of China's ancient sages. He lived from 551 to 479 BC, during the time of warfare and political upheavals known as the Spring and Autumn Period. He proposed a return to order by means of strict adherence to traditional precepts of correct behaviour at all levels of society.

Today the town of 200,000 is a major pilgrimage spot for adherents of the Confucian philosophy, especially during the annual festival held in September. Among the many Confucian sites in Qufu, the most significant are **Kong Ling (Tomb of Confucius)**, **Kong Miao (Confucian Temple)**, **Dacheng Tang (Dacheng Hall)** and **Kong Fu (Kong Family Mansion)**.

The Kong Miao takes up much of the central area of the town and is where Confucius taught his students. The temple was expanded in the years following Confucius' death. A series of courtyards each containing pavilions brings you to the heart of the compound. Here you'll find the Dacheng Tang, a splendid 32m (105ft) tall hall used by visitors to present gifts to Confucius.

Next to the temple, the Kong Fu was the extensive residence of the descendants of the great man. It is a mix of administrative, devotional and residential buildings.

150km (93 miles) south of Jinan.
Open: all the sights open 8am–5pm.
Admission charge to all sights.

Gate of the Residence of the Saint in the Confucius Mansions

Walk: Qingdao

The old town of Qingdao is easily covered on foot, but be ready for some hills.

This walk is about 6km (4 miles) long. Allow about 2 hours, not including time spent visiting the sights included.

Begin your walk at Huashi Lou, just east of Di Er Haibin (Number Two Bathing Beach).

1 Huashi Lou

This was once the German governor's fishing retreat, mixing Teutonic and Greek styles. If you climb to the turret at the top, the views are superb. If you detour inland you'll find the Badaguan neighbourhood where colonial villas remain splendid on tree-lined streets.

18 Huanghai. Tel: (0532) 8387 2168. Open: 7am–5pm. Admission charge.

Walk west along the beachside Nanhai until the first beach of Number Two Bathing Beach.

2 Di Er Haibin (Number Two Bathing Beach)

This is more secluded and quiet than the Number One Bathing Beach, where you'll be offered everything from speedboat trips to seafood kebabs.

Continue along the coast, now on Laiyang. On your right, where Yushan meets Laiyang, is Xiaoyushan Park.

3 Xiaoyushan Gongyuan (Xiaoyushan Park)

This park is quiet, verdant and steep, with a small pagoda on top.

Continue on Yushan and turn right on Longkou. At this historical part of the German concession, you soon reach the Protestant Church on your right.

4 Jidu Jiaotang (Protestant church)

Also known as Christ Church, the interior is of the austere style favoured by Lutherans, although some beautiful stained-glass windows have been restored since attacks during the Cultural Revolution.

Turn right after the church and you soon reach Xinhaoshan Park, and to the right the Ying Binguan.

5 Ying Binguan

This is the former German governor's residence and is now a good museum.

Open: 8am–5pm. Admission charge.

Return to Longkou, across Jiangsu and

turn right onto Jining. Ahead on your left is Tianzhu Jiaotang (St Michael's Catholic Church).

6 Tianzhu Jiaotang (St Michael's Catholic church)

The church is an imposing twin-spired edifice. The surrounding area is quite lively and includes a busy fish market.

Open: Mon–Sat 8am–5pm. Admission charge unless you are attending Mass.

Walk downhill on any of the small lanes through fascinating neighbourhoods and you'll soon reach Zhongshan Lu.

7 Zhongshan (Zhongshan Street)

This is Qingdao's main shopping street, with department stores of little interest to the visitor, although there are good restaurants and a few handicrafts galleries.

Turn left on Zhongshan and walk towards the beach. After crossing Taiping, walk along the Zhanqiao Pier.

8 Huilan Ge (Huilan Pavilion) and Zhanqiao Pier

Walk along the Zhanqiao Pier (*Open: 7am–5pm. Admission charge*) to Huilan Pavilion, Qingdao's icon, which graces every bottle of the city's famous beer.

From here you can walk along the coast to your starting point at Huashi Lou.

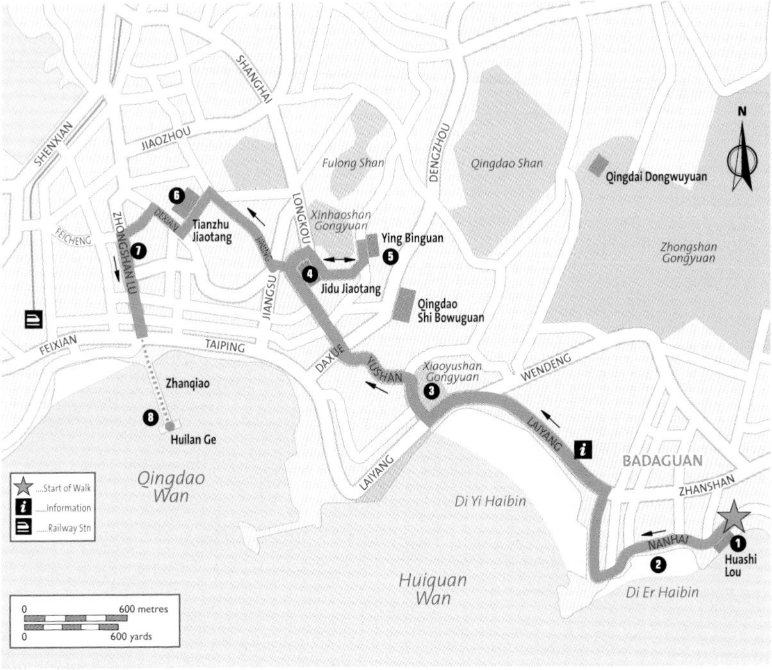

Dayunhe (Grand Canal)

At 1,800km (1,118 miles), the Grand Canal is the longest artificial waterway in the world. It stretches from Hangzhou to Beijing, passing through Suzhou and Wuxi in Central China and Shandong and Hebei provinces in the North. Passing through the mountains of Shandong Province it reaches a height of 42m (138ft), its greatest height. The canal's average width is 30m (98½ft). At present it is not possible to navigate the entire length, but this may change as China takes steps to reopen the canal fully for commerce and tourism.

Originally the brainchild of Fu Chai, the Duke of Wu (present-day Suzhou), and seen as a quick way of transporting troops and supplies north, construction began in the 5th century BC to facilitate the transport of rice from the Yangtze Valley to Beijing. During succeeding centuries, rivers and lakes were linked by artificial stretches of waterway to create the whole. The Grand Canal was fully opened in the early 7th century AD and provided the main connection between North and South China.

Since the 10th century, boats travelling along the canal have been able to negotiate the varying elevations along the route by using an elaborate lock system developed during the Song Dynasty.

Although at times it has served as an artery for military adventure, the

Parts of the Grand Canal continue to be used some 1,500 years after it was constructed

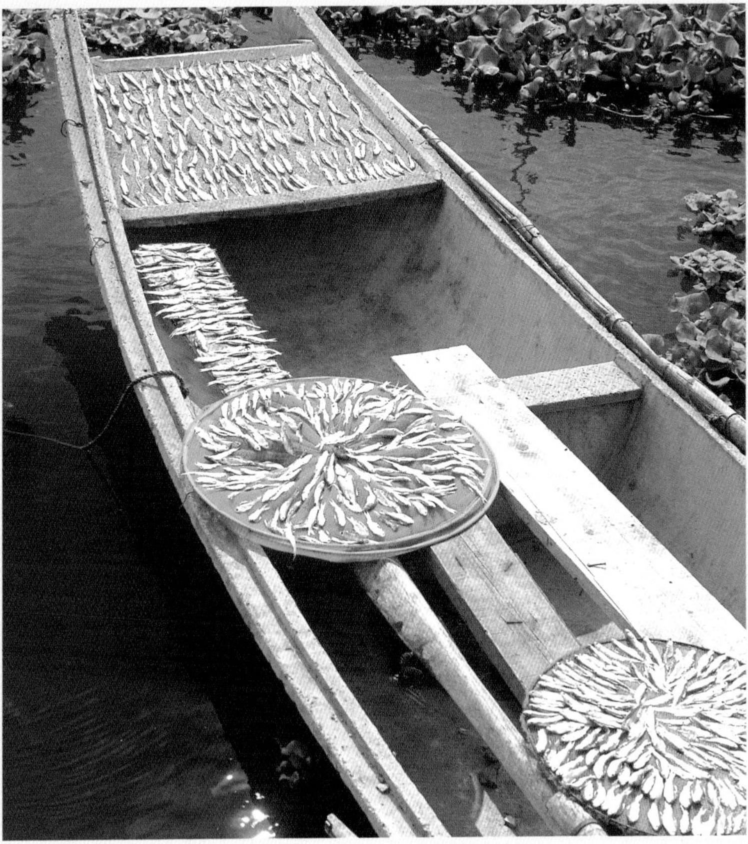

Moving fish stalls ply sections of the canal

canal's primary use has been peaceful. During imperial times its main purpose was to transport grain from the southern and central regions to the capital, and at its zenith as many as 8,000 boats conveyed between 250,000 and 360,000 tonnes of grain every year to Beijing.

Silting, combined with the growth of railways, saw the decline of the historical waterway. The canal stayed in use in stretches, and on a smaller scale. In places, houses were built on what had been its bed.

Despite the advent of cruise tourism along the Hangzhou to Yangzhou stretch, this waterway has remained a muddy mess. Yet it traverses beautiful countryside and some lovely cities, offering a glimpse of a time when imperial barges and grain boats plied its route.

West of Beijing

This section covers Gansu and Shaanxi provinces. At a site a few kilometres outside Xian, China first became a single country during the Qin Dynasty (221–206 BC) – in fact the name we use for the country is probably derived from the name of that dynasty. This site, then known as Chang'an, meaning 'Eternal Peace', remained the capital of China for seven centuries throughout the Han, Sui and the Tang dynasties.

Gansu Province, to the north and west of Shaanxi, has a cultural heritage dating to Neolithic times, and many important sights on the fabled Silk Road.

LANZHOU

The largest city and capital of Gansu Province lies along the old Silk Road on the upper Yellow River near the Great Wall, in a region of mountains and deserts. Strategically located in a narrow gorge, the city dominates all traffic between China's remote Northwest and Central China. Consequently Lanzhou is a staging post for rail journeys to the north and west, with a connection to Urumqi (in the vast and sparsely populated Xinjiang Autonomous Region), and onward to Kazakhstan. Lanzhou stands at an altitude of 1,600m (5,249ft).

Baita Shan (White Pagoda Hill)

The pagoda on the hill dates from the 14th-century Yuan Dynasty, but has been restored several times. It is octagonal, has seven storeys and is 17m (56ft) high. The hill is a forested park with other pavilions and temples and provides excellent views of the city below.

North bank of the river, near the Zhongshan Bridge. A cable car crosses the Yellow River just north of the Zhongshan Bridge. Open: 6am–6pm.

Gansu Sheng Bowuguan (Gansu Provincial Museum)

A silver-chased plate depicting the Greek god Bacchus, dating from the 2nd century BC, provides some evidence of the kind of goods that moved in an eastward direction along the Silk Road. The museum's exhibits are otherwise firmly Chinese, including a vast display of Neolithic pottery and the famous Flying Horse of Gansu, galloping on the wings of a swallow, dating from the Eastern Han period (AD 25–220) that was found in a nearby tomb. There is also a good section devoted to the natural history of the area.

Xijin Xi. Tel: (0930) 232 5049.
Open: Mon–Sat 9am–5pm. Closed: Sun.
Admission charge.

Wuquan Gongyuan (Five Springs Park)

The park stands at the foot of 2,000m (6,562ft) high Lanshan Mountain, the summit of which can be reached by a 20-minute cable-car ride. The park itself is dotted with temples and waterfalls, and retains a sense of wild drama despite the man-made elements.
Jiuquan. Open: 6am–5pm.
Admission charge.

XIAN

Emperor Qin Shi Huang ordered the creation of the Terracotta Army, one of China's most fascinating sights on a site, then known as Chang'an, meaning 'Eternal Peace', which remained the capital of China for seven centuries throughout the Han, Sui and the Tang dynasties. Shaanxi's relevance continued into the modern era, when

(*continued on p110*)

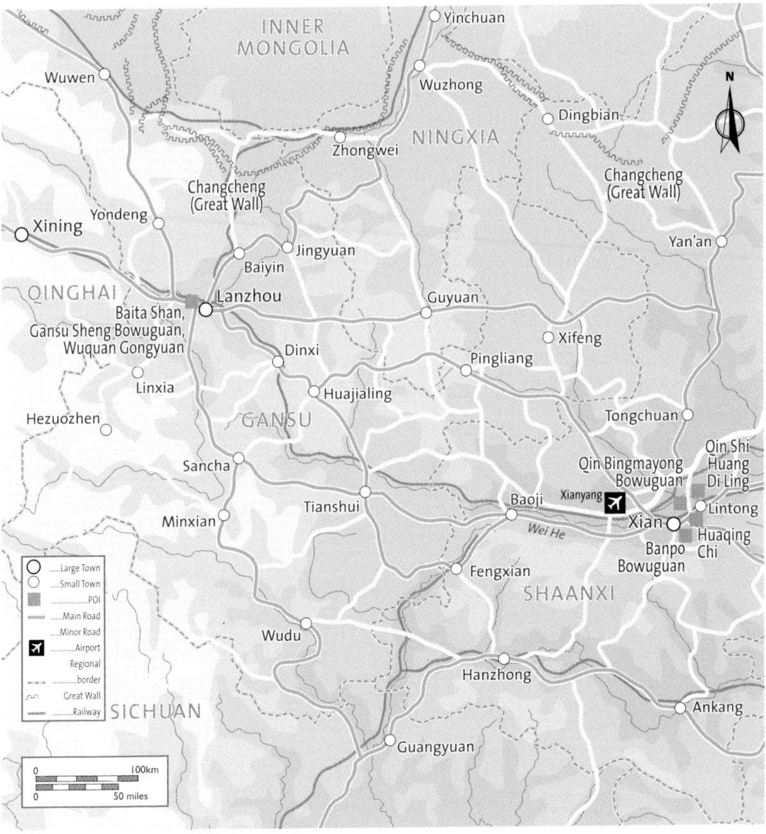

Marco Polo and the Silk Route

Marco Polo (1254–1324) was a Venetian merchant and traveller whose account of his adventures in China, and at the court of the Mongol Emperor Kublai Khan, became the subject of one of the greatest of all travel books. As a result, aristocratic Europe became entranced with China and with Chinese products such as silk and porcelain.

Marco Polo's father and uncle had already made one trading visit to Kublai Khan's court at Beijing, whose splendour was legendary. When they decided to return to China in 1271, they took the young Marco with them. Kublai Khan took him into his service as an envoy, and finally as governor of Yangzhou. Marco Polo left China in 1292, returning to Venice in 1295 and writing *Il Milione* (*The Million*, translated as *The Travels of Marco Polo*).

Some scholars have questioned whether Marco ever reached China. While much of his narrative describes real people, places and conditions in China at the time, there are glaring

Marco Polo sailed from Venice to the court of Kublai Khan

Families still travel the Silk Route, staying in tents en route

omissions, such as the Great Wall, foot-binding, printing, tea and the Chinese script. Names are frequently given in Persian, raising the suspicion that his 'journey' was actually made through the pages of a contemporary Persian account, augmented by tales heard from Arabic traders.

Silk Route

Arabic traders would have reached China by means of the ancient Silk Route, linking Europe with the Far East by way of Central Asia. There were several branches to the route, but from the 2nd century AD onwards, the two most popular ran from the Kaiyuanmen Gate in Xian (called Chang'an at the time), across the Gobi Desert to Turpan, Tashkent and Samarkand (the summer route), or Kashgar and Bactria (the winter route), and thence to Baghdad and the Mediterranean.

Products and cultural ideas flowed in both directions. The main Chinese export was silk, which was highly prized by the emperors and wealthy citizens of ancient Rome. Imports included cotton, grapes and, more lastingly, the Buddhist religion, imported from India.

Nowadays, the fabled Silk Route exercises an irresistible appeal to visitors from all over the world. Where journeys in the past may have taken months, if not years, today these same journeys can be completed in a matter of days. With this burgeoning interest, both major and minor sights along China's Silk Route are being rapidly restored. Now they will not be welcoming merchants, but curious travellers.

Mao Zedong's Communists established their base in Yenan.

Banpo Bowuguan (Banpo Neolithic Village Museum)

This 6,500-year-old village is of interest to scholars of the Yangshao culture as well as tourists, and visitors are permitted to walk among the remains of the villagers' huts. Weapons, tools, farming and fishing implements are on display.

Banpo. In the eastern suburbs, across the Chanhe River. Tel: (029) 8353 2482. Open: 9am–5pm. Admission charge.

Chengqiang (City wall)

The city's powerful 14th-century Ming Dynasty wall, with its moats, towers and gates, has been restored, thus recreating some of the glory of Xian's past. It is an impressive 12m (40ft) high monument to the city's former importance. There are four great fortified gates: Beimen (North Gate), Nanmen (South Gate), Dongmen (East Gate) and Ximen (West Gate). The walls are ringed by Huancheng Jie (itself divided into quarters called Bei, Nan, Dong and Xi).

Xian's city wall was built by the Ming emperors

XIAN'S MUSLIM MINORITY

Xian has 15 mosques, including the Great Mosque, to cater for its population of 60,000 or so Muslims, known as Hui, who are ethnically indistinguishable from the Han. The Hui are descended from the merchants and traders of the Silk Road, which, for centuries, was the only reliable route for transporting China's commodities to Persia, the Middle East and even to Europe. The old Muslim quarter is a colourful, lively and friendly part of the town, with shops and street restaurants jostling together in narrow alleyways around the Great Mosque.

Da Qingzhen Si (Great Mosque)

Set amid the rambling and jumbled alleys of Xian's old Muslim quarter, the mosque, founded in AD 742, is an interesting example of how traditional Islamic architectural and decorative styles adapted to China – mostly being dominated by the Chinese forms. A bewildering array of architectural styles almost belies its status as an Islamic shrine, but Xian's Muslim population attends religiously. The prayer hall, at the far end of the interior garden, is not accessible to non-Muslims.

Huajue Xiang, west of the Drum Tower in the city centre's old Muslim quarter. Tel: (029) 8721 9807. Open: 8am–6pm. Admission charge.

Da Yan Ta (Big Wild Goose Pagoda)

This pagoda gained its curious name from the legend that a nearby temple was built to honour a sacred goose. The pagoda dates from AD 652, but was recently rebuilt. At 64m (210ft), it is 21m (69ft) higher than the Small Wild Goose Pagoda and its seven storeys and 284 interior steps lead to a fine viewpoint.
Yanta, about 2 km (1¼ miles) outside the old city walls near the History Museum. Tel: (029) 8525 3802. Open: 8.30am–6pm. Admission charge.

Gulou (Drum Tower)

Drums were beaten from here at night as the city gates were about to close. Built in 1380, the tower is 34m (111½ft) high.
Beiyuanmen, between the Great Mosque and the Bell Tower. Tel: (029) 8727 4580. Open: 8.30am–5pm. Admission charge.

Shaanxi Lishi Bowuguan (Shaanxi Historical Museum)

This superb new building is big enough – as it has to be – to do justice to the vast archaeological zone that much of Shaanxi seems to be, particularly the area around Xian (formerly Chang'an). A vast range of objects from all periods is on display, and even the famous Terracotta warriors are no more than an element in a long and fascinating story.
Xiaozhai, near the Big Wild Goose Pagoda. Tel: (029) 8521 9422. Open: 8.30am–5.30pm (summer); 9am–4.30pm (winter). Admission charge.

Xiao Yan Ta (Small Wild Goose Pagoda)

As its name implies, this is a smaller cousin to the Big Wild Goose Pagoda, having lost its top two storeys to an earthquake in the 16th century. Still 43m (141ft) high, it is a graceful structure dating from the early 7th century, which may be climbed for its view (*see p113*).
Youyi Xi, south of Nanmen Gate. Tel: (029) 8525 3455. Open: 8.30am–5pm. Admission charge.

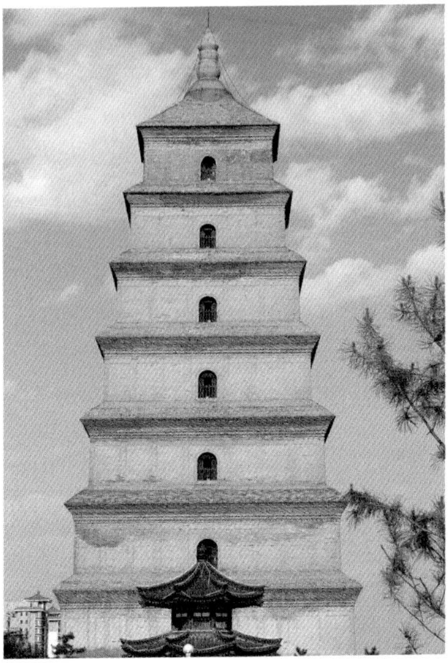

The Big Wild Goose Pagoda

Tour: Xian city

A big and not especially attractive city but with some superb monuments scattered around, Xian is probably best toured through a combination of walking, taxi and pedicab.

Allow 4 hours.

Begin at the North Gate.

1 Beimen (North Gate)
The 14km (8½-mile) long city wall dates from the 14th century and is built on earlier Tang foundations. This gate is one of four set at the principal compass points.
It is best to go by taxi along Beida, then right into Lianhu to Lianhu Park.

2 Lianhu Gongyuan (Lianhu Park)
Parks are not numerous in Xian, although many avenues are lined with trees. This slight detour passes among the lakes and greenery before re-emerging on to the fuming streets.
Come out onto Honghu, Beiguangji and right into Xiyang to the Great Mosque and its small alleyways.

3 Da Qingzhen Si (Great Mosque)
The mosque (*see p110*) is a relaxed and welcoming place after fighting the souvenir stalls, and an appropriately tranquil refuge from the outside world.
Continue on Xiyang and turn right to the Drum Tower.

4 Gulou (Drum Tower)
(*See p111.*)
Continue south of the Drum Tower and turn left onto Xida to the Bell Tower.

5 Zhonglou (Bell Tower)
There is a notable view from this centrally located point (*see p116*).
Come south into Nanda and left into Dongmutoushi, then turning right for the Forest of Stone Stelae.

6 Beilin Bowuguan (Forest of Stone Stelae)
This remarkable collection consists of ancient writings and calligraphy carved on thousands of stone tablets. The content is of most interest to scholars, but the setting in an old Confucian temple, which is now a museum, means that non-specialists can enjoy the sight.
15 Sanxue Jie. Tel: (029) 8725 8448.
Open: 8.30am–6.30pm.
Admission charge.
Take Shuyuanmen St west to the South Gate.

7 Nanmen (South Gate)

This is another of the four principal gateways in the Ming-era walls, marking the boundary of the old city (*see p110*).

It is probably best to go by taxi or pedicab to Youyi Xi and the Small Wild Goose Pagoda.

8 Xiao Yan Ta (Small Wild Goose Pagoda)

The 7th-century pagoda's 15 tiers gradually diminish in size as they ascend above the grounds of the Jianfu Temple to its summit (*see p111*).

A taxi or pedicab is essential for the next leg to the Big Wild Goose Pagoda.

9 Da Yan Ta (Big Wild Goose Pagoda)

Dating from the 7th century, this is the better of the two pagodas to climb as it offers better views (*see p111*).

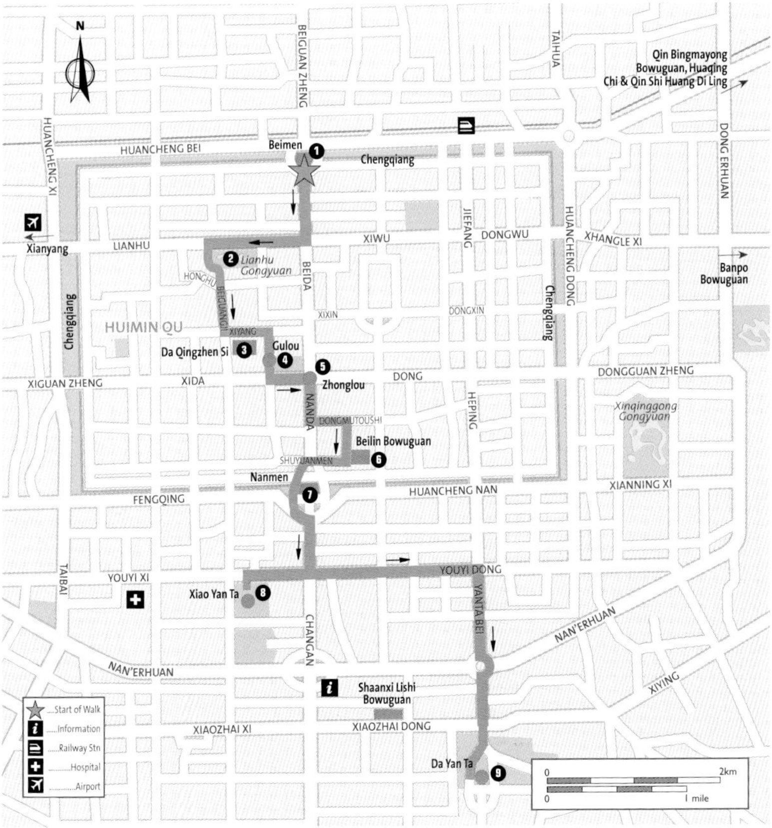

Inventions

It seems ironic that so many of China's difficulties with colonial powers in the 19th century were caused by its inferior technology because China has a proud record of innovation stretching back for centuries. Practical and widespread application of the products, however, was lacking.

Gunpowder, the world's oldest explosive, a mixture of sulphur, charcoal and saltpetre, was in use in China as early as the 10th century during the Song Dynasty, when it was used in grenades and rockets, and later in firearms. Another invention, which revolutionised warfare in its time, was the stirrup, which permitted greater power in the delivery of a lance blow.

The crossbow, an even earlier military advance, was first documented in China around the 4th century BC. Sun Tzu's important book *The Art of War* refers to giant crossbows and their use.

The magnetic compass ...

… and gunpowder are both Chinese innovations

Peaceful processes

Paper-making and block-printing were more peaceable. Paper was in use by the 2nd century AD, and there are indications that it may have been invented as early as the 2nd century BC. The earliest known printed book (AD 868), using the woodblock method, is a Buddhist Diamond Sutra. Although clocks and sundials had been known to people for millennia, revolutionary developments in mechanical clocks using the escapement mechanism came from 11th-century China. The wheelbarrow can be traced to 2nd-century Han Dynasty times and is often seen in tomb murals of that period. The suspension bridge dates to an even earlier time, the 3rd century BC, with examples in both China and Tibet. The pound lock, used with such success throughout the world's canal systems today, was first developed during the Song Dynasty (960–1279) and put to great effect on the Dayunhe (Grand Canal). Piston bellows, developed so enthusiastically during Europe's 18th-century Industrial Revolution, were being used in ancient China as early as the 3rd century BC.

China also gave the world kites, porcelain, the magnetic compass and even a pre-vaccination form of immunisation against smallpox. Then there are noodles, and tea, whose cultivation and consumption began in China.

Zhonglou (Bell Tower)

The tower where the bell was rung to signify the opening of the city gates, now offering a fine view of the busy city, dates from 1384. It incorporates an antique store with carved beams and a beautifully painted ceiling. Equally notable is the fact that the 14th-century wooden tower hangs together without the help of nails.
Nanda. Tel: (029) 8721 4665.
Open: 8.30am–5pm. Admission charge.

XIAN ENVIRONS

Huaqing Chi (Huaqing Hot Springs)

This superb thermal springs complex lies not far away from the location of the Terracotta Army site, some 30km (18½ miles) east of Xian. The pools, bathhouses and garden pavilions are being restored to their Tang Dynasty glory, when this was a favoured resort of emperors.

The famous 'Xian incident' occurred here in 1936. At this historic event, the nationalist leader Chiang Kai Shek was held prisoner by his generals until he agreed to form an alliance with the Communists against Japanese invaders.
Lintong County. Minibuses on the way to the Terracotta Army site can stop here.
Open: 8am–7pm. Admission charge.

Qin Bingmayong Bowuguan (Qin Terracotta Army Museum)

Many visitors will consider this UNESCO World Heritage Site to be the most fascinating sight in China. As recently as 1974, there was nothing here. That year some peasants digging a well chanced upon an awesome scene. They broke through an underground vault where they discovered 6,000 life-size figures of terracotta soldiers and horses in battle array, each face different – an eternal imperial guard for the founder of the Qin Dynasty, the Emperor Qin Shi Huang, whose still unopened tomb is nearby.

Two more vaults filled with terracotta warriors have since been uncovered and opened to the public, one of them a 'command post' for the buried legions. To date, excavations have revealed a total of 8,099 life-size terracotta figures. Archaeologists believe other such pits await discovery. Not only life size, the figures are incredibly life-like. Archers kneeling to shoot, guards at attention, cavalry astride their steeds, all ready to protect the emperor in the afterlife. While the claim that none is identical is

A terracotta warrior in full battle array

exaggerated, there are visible variations in the armour and physical appearances of the soldiers.

The scene inside the vaults is charged with mystery, as visitors come face to face with the silent army. Unfortunately, they also come face to face with a far from silent army of fellow visitors, a shuffling queue that gives you little chance to stop and admire the sight (photography is also forbidden). However, there is not much the museum curators can do about the number of tourists eager to see the buried army, and they do their best to accommodate them.

Also worth visiting at the site of the tomb is a small air-conditioned museum displaying important finds from the Terracotta Army and surrounding area, most notably two fine bronze chariots and horses, and examples of Qin Dynasty weaponry.
Lintong County. Located 40km (25 miles) northeast of Xian.
Open: 9am–5pm. Admission charge.

The impressive site of the Terracotta Army

Qin Shi Huang Di Ling (Tomb of Qin Shi Huang Di)

The Emperor Qin Shi Huang, who ruled from 221 BC until his death in 209 BC, succeeded in uniting China, bringing the Warring States period to an end. Yet it is for his mausoleum and the nearby buried army of terracotta warriors (*see above*) that he is best known. The mausoleum's inner sanctuary is 2.5km (1½ miles) in circumference, and the outer boundary stretches for 6km (3¾ miles). Archaeologists have postponed its complete excavation and opening to the public, but it is possible to climb the 40m (131ft) high tumulus and ponder the life and times of the megalomaniac ruler buried beneath.

Contemporary historians wrote that the emperor was entombed with great quantities of treasure amid a bejewelled model of the heavens, representations of China's rivers flowing with mercury, and assorted crossbows and other booby traps designed to repel tomb raiders. As an added precaution, many of the artisans who laboured on the tomb were entombed with the emperor – taking their secrets to the grave.
Lintong County, 1.5km (1 mile) from the Qin Terracotta Army Museum.
Open: 9am–5pm. Admission charge.

The Long March

Mao Zedong (1893–1976) led the Communist revolution in China that, in 1949, added one-fifth of the human race to the roster of nations grouped under the red banner. Few individuals match so perfectly with their time and place to have such a major impact on the world. Chairman Mao, the first red emperor of China, born into a farming family in Hunan Province, was one such individual.

Today, Mao's portrait is no longer ubiquitous, and his 'little Red Book', *The Thoughts of Chairman Mao*, is a long way down the bestseller lists, but Mao still commands respect from ordinary Chinese. This is evident in the way the crowds shuffle respectfully past his embalmed body at his mausoleum in Beijing.

After graduating from a teacher training college in Changsha, Mao moved to Beijing where, in 1921, he became a founding member of the Chinese Communist Party. In 1923, the Communists forged an alliance with the Nationalists, and together the 'united front' consolidated power in Southern and Central China. In 1926, however, the alliance ended in armed conflict and the Communists were driven out of their strongholds. Mao learned two lessons from this: that guerrilla tactics were the way forward; and that 'political power grows through the barrel of a gun'.

A dramatic representation of soldiers and peasants celebrating the Long March

Mao's leadership of the Long March made him a figure of legend and authority

Mao settled in Jiangxi Province, where he set up a series of Communist bases, but the Nationalists were determined to destroy their former allies. In October 1934, Nationalist forces drove Mao and his followers from the province, and thus began the Long March or, as the Chinese refer to it, the Great March of the Red Army.

Trekking more than 9,500km (5,903 miles) across China, with some 86,000 men, Mao intended to find a new and more secure base in Shaanxi Province from which to pursue his 'people's war'. The epic march, across some of the roughest country on earth, took a year, and only 6,000 of his troops survived. The new base chosen by Mao Zedong, Zhou Enlai and other senior leaders of the Chinese Communist Party was in the remote loess country around Yan'an. Here, the survivors of Mao's First Red Army were joined by survivors of the Second and Fourth Red Armies in a secure base area beyond the reach of Chiang Kai Shek's Nationalist forces, themselves increasingly threatened by the advancing forces of Imperial Japan. The Long March was successfully completed in October 1935, and the Communist Party leadership, by now dominated by Mao, began reorganising its forces for the long and successful three-way fight against both the Kuomintang and the Japanese. It was from this secure stronghold in Yan'an that the People's Liberation Army (PLA) would eventually emerge some 14 years later to take control of the entire Chinese mainland and establish the People's Republic of China in 1949.

Getting away from it all

No country that occupies such a vast area as China could be short of places renowned for natural beauty. Chinese poets and painters have always placed great emphasis on their land's scenic wonders, as though beauty to delight the senses and inspire the mind was part of the compact between the Middle Kingdom and the Heaven that watched over it.

The 'Destination guide' will have led you to some oases of tranquillity, even in the midst of huge cities. The lakes of Beijing and the coastlines near Dalian and Qingdao offer respite from urban stress and the fascinating but sometimes frenetic visits to historical sights. The sacred mountains of Northern China, Wutai Shan (*pp90–91*) and Song Shan (*pp95–7*) can be quite relaxing if you have the time to explore at leisure. This section takes you further afield, from the grasslands of Inner Mongolia and the distant reaches of the Silk Road to a volcanic lake on the border of North Korea in Jilin Province.

NEI MENGGU (INNER MONGOLIA)

Two-thirds of Inner Mongolia consists of the broad grasslands from which the Mongol hordes of Genghis Khan sprang forth to rampage across China, the Middle East and Europe in the 13th century. The remainder is desert and mountain. Today, Inner Mongolia (as distinct from the independent Republic of Mongolia to the north) is an autonomous region of China. Some descendants of the horsemen of the grasslands still live in compressed sheep's wool tents called *gher* (yurts), but these symbols of the ancient way of life survive largely as part of a burgeoning tourist industry. Most Mongolians, who are outnumbered

Clear water and peaks that touch the clouds

The splendid modern tomb of Mongol warrior Genghis Khan at Ejin Horo Qi

five-to-one by Han Chinese and other nationalities, prefer to ride motorbikes and live in ordinary houses.

Hohhot

The capital of Inner Mongolia, Hohhot is a base for tours of the grasslands, which involve visiting a rural community and sleeping in a yurt. **Nei Menggu Bowuguan (Inner Mongolia Museum)** (*2 Xinhua. Tel: (0471) 691 8772. Open: 9am–5pm. Admission charge*) has notable displays depicting the traditional lifestyle of the Mongolian people. Other points of interest in the city are **Qingzhen Da Si (Great Mosque)** (*28 Tongdao Bei. Open: Sat–Thur. Free admission*), dating from the Ming Dynasty, and **Wuta Si (Five Pagoda Temple)** (*Wutasi Hou. Open: 8am–6pm. Admission charge*).

Beyond Hohhot

At Ejin Horo Qi, southwest of Hohhot near Dongsheng, **Chengji Sihan Lingyuan (Genghis Khan Mausoleum)** (*Open: 7am–7pm. Admission charge*) is a beautiful modern building, with its elegant domed roof pavilions. Whether or not it is really Genghis Khan who lies beneath, who can say?

Hailaer is the northernmost major town in Inner Mongolia and an excellent starting point for a trip (on horseback if you wish) to visit the grasslands.

Hohhot is a 1-hour flight, or 10-hour train or bus trip, from Beijing. Flights from Xian take 1½ hours. Hailaer is a 2½-hour flight from Hohhot, or 2 hours directly from Beijing.

QINGHAI

Qinghai Province is west of Gansu, and the provincial capital of Xining is only three hours by road from Lanzhou. The new Beijing to Lhasa express train also stops at Xining. **Qinghai Hu (Qinghai Lake)**, China's largest saltwater lake, is surrounded by snow-tipped mountains and located 3,200m (10,500ft) above sea level. The **Niao Dao (Bird Island)** sanctuary hosts about 100,000 migrating birds, including geese, cranes, vultures and Mongolian larks. Its Longbao Black-Necked Crane Sanctuary plays an important role in the preservation of this threatened species.

China's minority peoples often retain their distinctive style of dress

Xining is a 4-hour flight from Beijing. To arrive by bus, start from Lanzhou in Gansu Province, 3 hours distant. There is no public transport to Qinghai Lake – arrange a tour from Xining.

CHANGBAI SHAN ZIRAN BAOHUQU (EVER-WHITE MOUNTAIN NATURE RESERVE)

Trees are the main players at this pristine sight in Jilin Province, on the border with North Korea, where virgin forest is protected as a UNESCO Biosphere Reserve. Changbai Shan is China's largest National Park with an area of 1,965sq km (760sq miles).

The trees form bands of growth, depending on the altitude, and include white birch, Korean pine, dragon spruce and fir. Above 2,000m (6,562ft), the landscape is tundra, while in the valleys there are deciduous trees that attract tour groups for their autumnal colours. The area is also famed for its medicinal herbs, notably ginseng.

The highlight of a trip to Changbai Shan is a visit to the deep blue **Tian Chi Lake (Heaven's Lake** – one of many so-named lakes in China), which is the crater of a dormant volcano that last erupted in 1702, and the deepest lake in China. The lake has an altitude of 2,189m (7,182ft) and a circumference of 13km (8½ miles). The border with North Korea runs through the middle of the lake. There are numerous hot springs in the area and an impressive waterfall cascades from the lake.

Qinghai Lake, at the foot of towering mountains

The northern slope of the mountain is the most heavily visited since it is the access route to the lake. There is a road as far as the waterfall, but after that you're on your own to reach the lake. The nearby border with North Korea is not clearly marked, so don't stray too far since North Korea is not a place you would enjoy visiting.
560km (347 miles) east of Changchun, the capital of Jilin Province. Due to heavy snowfalls, the park is only open from June to September.

XINJIANG

The Xinjiang Uighur Autonomous Region, China's largest and westernmost region, has a population of about 13 million and shares borders with several former Soviet republics as well as Mongolia, Afghanistan and Pakistan. The Uighurs are one of China's national minorities, a people of Turkic origin, mostly settled in Xinjiang, a territory that they share with 12 other minorities, including the Hui, Tajiks, Mongols and Kazakhs. This region is the heart of the Silk Road in China, and the otherwise forbidding desert is dotted with verdant oases.

Kashgar

A fabled city on the Silk Route, Kashgar (called Kashi by the Chinese, and shown by this name on most maps) is about as far west, and as isolated, as you can get in China. A three-day bus ride from Urumqi leads to Kashgar's **Jiari Jishi (Sunday Market)** and the impressive **Qingzhen Si (Id Kah Mosque)**. More realistically, it's seven hours by air from Beijing, with a stop

Dramatic landscape in the Turpan Depression

in Urumqi. From Kashgar, it is possible to leave China by bus, or preferably by chartered four-wheel-drive vehicle, and travel into either Kyrgyzstan or to the Pakistani capital of Islamabad via the famous Karakoram Highway. **Karakul Lake** is a beautiful spot on the Karakoram Highway 200km (120 miles) from Kashgar. Tour agencies in Kashgar can arrange overnight trips.

Remote, unique and astonishing – yet only 40km (25 miles) from downtown Kashgar – **Tushuk Tash (Shipton's Arch)** (named after its discoverer, a British diplomat) is believed to be by far the largest natural rock arch anywhere in the world. The height of the opening is 366m (1,200ft) – five times the height of Rainbow Bridge in Utah, the highest natural arch in the Americas.

Kashgar is a 2-hour flight from Urumqi, or 24 hours by train or bus.

Turpan

This former oasis city on the Silk Road is best known for the nearby **Turpan Depression**, 154m (505ft) below sea level, the lowest point geographically in China. The town of Turpan is hot but idyllic, with grape trellis covering the vehicle-free streets.

The surrounding oases and desert contain the ruins of two ancient cities, Jiaohe, also known as Yarkhoto, and Gaochang, also known as Karakhoja. To the west of Turpan the ruins of **Jiaohe** (*10km/6 miles west of Turpan. Open: 9am–6pm. Admission charge*), originally a Han garrison town, are the most accessible of the ancient Silk Road cities in Xinjiang. The city eventually became part of the Gaochang Kingdom. The well-preserved ruins stand on a hill that was once an island surrounded by two small rivers; the rivers have long since dried up. **Gaochang** (*46km/29 miles southeast of Turpan. Open: 8.30am–6pm. Admission charge*) was developed as a garrison town by the Chinese following the Han capture of the region in the 2nd century BC. The city prospered during the Tang Dynasty (618–907), but subsequently went into decline. It was abandoned early in the 14th century. The ruins that remain today date mainly from the Tang Era.

Turpan is on the Silk Road, 200km (124 miles) southeast of Urumqi, a 3-hour bus ride.

Urumqi

The capital of Xinjiang, this city of 1 million people can be reached by train from Beijing. An undistinguished city set in the fabulously wild terrain along which the Silk Route once wound its way, Urumqi has a good museum, the **Xinjiang Weiwuer Zizhiqu Bowuguan (Xinjiang Autonomous Region Museum)** (*132 Xibei. Tel: (0991) 453 6536. Open: 10am–1.30pm, 3.30–6.30pm. Admission charge*). This is an excellent museum focusing on the Silk Road, with ancient mummies and Buddhist frescoes, as well as displays detailing the life of the region's minorities. **Tian Shan (Heavenly Mountain)** and **Tianchi (Heaven Lake)** are 115km (71½ miles) east of the city. The lake is perched at an altitude of 2,000m (6,562ft) and the weather can be bitterly cold, even in summer. The deep blue lake with a background on snow-capped mountains is superb.

Urumqi is 5 hours from Beijing by air, or 48 hours by train. From Xian, Urumqi is a 2-hour flight or a 24-hour train trip.

Tianchi Lake

When to go

Beijing and Northern China's climate can be compared to that of Europe, with four distinct seasons but with rainfall more likely in the summer, which can relieve the heat somewhat. It is not uncommon to see people wearing white surgical masks on the street during both winter and summer to protect their lungs from both the natural and man-made environmental pollution.

Beijing's maximum temperature in the summer reaches above 30°C (86°F), while in winter some days do not get above freezing. Beijing is also a windy city – the loess plateau north and west of the city deposits a fine layer of yellow dust during the summer and the deserts of Mongolia send frigid blasts during the winter. However, if you are well prepared, Beijing winters can be lovely – the lakes are frozen and light snowfalls dust the buildings. Still, the ideal time for a visit is either spring or autumn when the climate is at its most temperate. Given the choice, take autumn – the air is cleaner after the rains of summer. One caveat here, however – the major national holidays during the first week of May and the

WEATHER CONVERSION CHART

25.4mm = 1 inch

°F = 1.8 × °C + 32

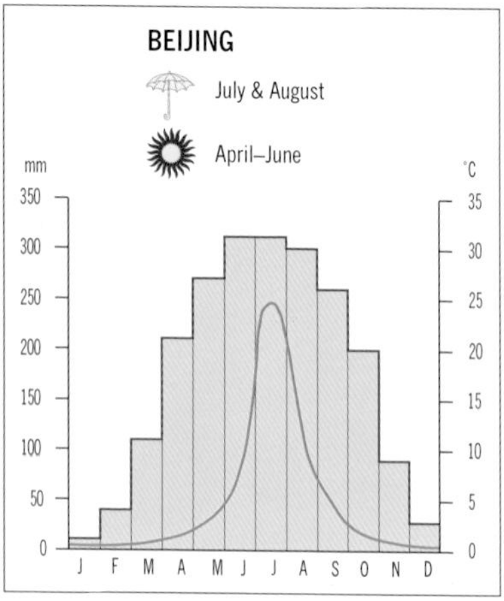

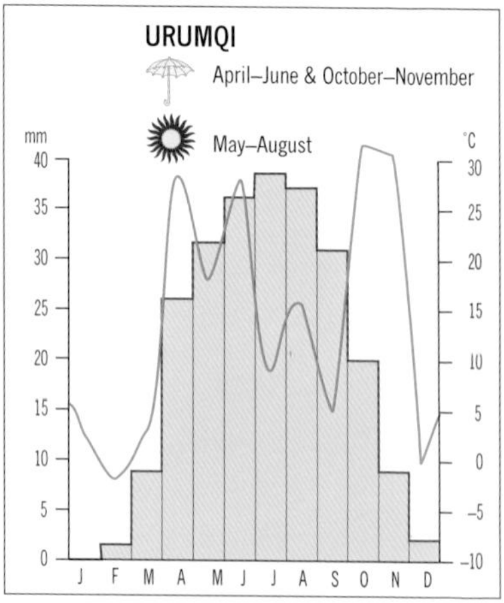

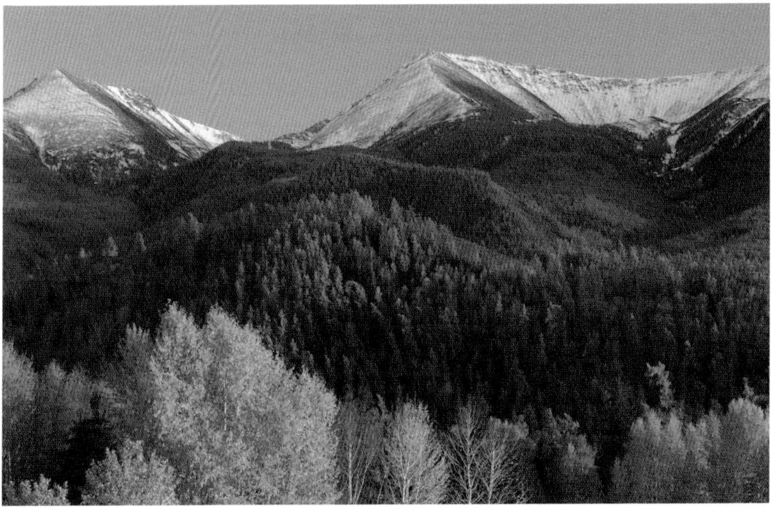

Spring and autumn are the best seasons to visit China

first week of October free the Chinese from their jobs and they take to the roads, rails and skies in vast numbers, making travel difficult. Still, if you are safely ensconced in a pre-booked hotel, it's a fun time for enjoying the festivities and people-watching.

The Northeast is well known for outrageously cold winters, sometimes reaching below –40°C (–40°F) in the winter. Summers are a little cooler than in Beijing and quite pleasant. Cities along the coast, such as Tianjin, Dalian and Qingdao, are generally less given to extremes of weather than inland, but expect more out of season rainfall. The Northwest is dry all year, but torrid in the summer and colder than Beijing in the winter. Xian has a climate quite similar to Beijing's.

Pollution is, of course, a problem in many parts of the country and, depending on the time of the year, it can ruin a holiday. The Hexi Corridor in Gansu Province with Lanzhou at its centre is one of the most polluted areas in the world. Lanzhou, according to *Time* magazine, was voted the 'World's Most Polluted City' in 1998.

Even in areas without much heavy industry, the timing of a visit is important. In far-flung Kashgar, the sudden arrival of colder winter weather can quickly see the previously cobalt blue skies haze over dramatically.

As with any destination, a modicum of luck is required. A perfectly clear winter's day walking around Beijing's Forbidden City can be one of life's greatest moments, a memory to treasure. Alternatively, rains can linger on into September anywhere in the country, disrupting an otherwise perfectly planned trip.

Getting around

Transportation systems and the infrastructure that supports them have improved greatly during the past few years; this is to be welcomed, given the long distances that need to be covered. Gone are the days of white-knuckle experiences in ageing Russian aircraft on domestic routes, and improved roads mean that travelling times by car or bus have been cut in half.

Beijing has a good and expanding underground and light rail mass transit system. Still, given the vast distances and sometimes forbidding terrain, coupled with the increased demand on all public travel systems by the newly mobile local population, all travel options can at times be a challenge to the visitor. Foreigners on organised tours should have few complaints about transport, although some tours and visits are liable to cancellation at short (or no) notice for reasons that are not always explained. The main problem for independent travellers will be the language barrier.

By air

Air China, the Chinese national carrier, has an excellent reputation for safety and efficiency. State of the art equipment and well-trained staff have led seasoned international travellers to compare it favourably to Western airlines. Air China operates domestic flights as well, as do a plethora of smaller Chinese airlines, notably the Shanghai-based China Eastern Airlines. Beijing's **Capital Airport** (*Tel: (010) 6454 1100. http://en.bcia.com.cn*) is the country's aviation epicentre, with flights to any city in China with an airport. Beijing airport added a massive new terminal in preparation for the 2008 Olympics and is connected to the city centre by a light rail system. Domestic air travel in China is not expensive by international standards – there are even some privately owned budget carriers. Booking as far in advance as possible will improve your chances of getting the best price.

THOMAS COOK'S CHINA

'The first real railway line in China was opened last September with unexpected *éclat*, between Tientsin [Tianjin], Taku and Tongshan. The length of the line is only eighty-six and a half miles [138km], but the success achieved is a great factor towards future development in this direction . . .'

From Cook's *Excursionist and Tourist Advertiser*, 14 December 1888.

A steam locomotive in northeast China

By train

Railways are China's arteries – the most economical, safe and reliable way of travelling long distances, and they are the choice of the Chinese themselves. Without the trains' lifeline, the country would suffer some kind of fatal seizure, although sometimes trying to get on a train might do the same for foreign travellers. It is important to have sharp elbows, a note in Chinese stating the ticket type desired, and a willingness to kowtow to the ticket clerk, who will pronounce with the finality of an emperor on your travel plans. Alternatively, ask your hotel concierge or a reliable travel agent to handle this for you. Avoid the touts selling tickets around the train stations.

Once you find the right platform in an overcrowded station, the rest should go smoothly. Riding soft class, or soft class sleeper, is a good way to travel in China; a closed door compartment contains four bunks and you have clean linen, curtains, and meals in a dining car. Hard class is something else – particularly a hard seat on a long-distance train, though a hard class sleeper can also be, well, hard – six bunks in an open compartment, stacked three high.

Virtually the entire country is connected to the rail network, including a recently opened line to Lhasa, the capital of Tibet. Modern express trains ply the 1,300km (808-mile) Beijing to Shanghai route in 12 hours of climate-controlled luxury. A trip from Beijing to Tianjin takes a little over an hour on another modern express route.

There are two train stations in Beijing: **Beijing Huochezhan (Beijing Train Station)** (*Tel: (010) 5101 9999*) located southeast of the Forbidden City; and the larger **Beijing Xizhan (Beijing West Train Station)** (*Tel: (010)*

Taxis in Beijing are easily identified

5182 6273) in the southwest of the city. The express train to Shanghai, as well as the Trans-Siberian Express, leave from the Beijing Train Station.

By metro

Beijing's rapid transit system (*ditie*) started life as a military transport route in 1965 during the Sino-Soviet rift – the plan was to transport citizen soldiers to repel the Russian hordes expected to attack from the west. With this pedigree, it is not surprising that the original line is not quite as luxurious as the slick new Metro in Shanghai. The second Beijing line, which follows the old city walls in a rectangular route, is more useful. Further additions have expanded the system to over 200km (130 miles) of track. Announcements and station signage is in both English and Chinese, and the system is useful as well as inexpensive for the visitor, although peak times are quite crowded.

Tianjin Metro currently runs two lines in the city and expects to complete another seven lines by the year 2010. Shenyang Metro is under construction and its first line is due to be completed by late 2009, with a second line by 2010. Xian is at present also expected to complete its own underground system as early as 2009.

By taxi or car hire

Taxis abound in Beijing and all other Chinese cities. Rates are not expensive and the meter should always be used – if the driver doesn't want to use the meter, get out of the taxi. No tipping is expected, and most drivers speak little or no English. Have your destination written in Chinese or show the driver a map with Chinese characters. Private car hire in China always includes a driver, since only foreigners with residence visas can obtain the requisite Chinese driver's licence.

By bus

Bus travel within a city is only useful if you truly know your route, since announcements and signage are in Chinese only. Long-distance buses are most useful to reach destinations not on the railway network. The advantages over trains is that bus departures are more frequent and bus stations easier to reach than train stations. There are at least four bus stations in Beijing and other large cities – one for each of the cardinal points of the compass, i.e. if your destination is north, look for the Northern Bus Station. Buses generally take less time than trains, especially on the many new improved roads across China. However, this convenience is purchased at the cost of comfort and safety. Driving standards are abysmal and accidents not uncommon. Even when you arrive safely, you'll often be shattered by recollections of the driver's use of the horn rather than the brakes. Long-distance buses entertain their passengers with high-volume kung-fu movies, which might not be to your taste.

By bicycle

For decades the bicycle was the major form of short-distance travel in China, and during those times, short distances were the only distances travelled by all except the élite. Now, as the Chinese move up the vehicular ladder commensurate with their economic well-being, the bicycle is becoming less common, at least in the cities. There are still dedicated bicycle lanes in most Chinese cities, but the increase in motorised traffic and its pollution makes cycling less fun for the visitor than it used to be. Nonetheless, it is a good way to survey the less congested parts of cities. The best technique is to stay close to other cyclists who know the unwritten rules of the road and be especially careful at intersections.

You will find pedicabs a convenient and original way to travel

Accommodation

Hotels in China present the full range of standards. Joint ventures with some of the world's leading hotel groups have led to the development of hotels in the major tourist and international business zones whose commitment to quality is impeccable. International chains such as Hyatt, Shangri-La, Mandarin and St Regis have all established flagship properties of extremely high standards, with prices to match.

Luxurious spas, in-room Jacuzzis, private butlers, décor by internationally renowned designers, and *haute cuisine* are all available for those wishing to open their wallets.

Just beneath such lofty citadels of the good life lies the domain of the locally managed high-end hotels. These still offer all the services and standards you would find at home, but without the polished service of the international chains. In the mid-range you can find perfectly acceptable places to spend a few nights, but nothing approaching luxury. There may be variable service, lacking to absent foreign language skills, and the occasional unpleasant surprise of noisy neighbours and leaky taps. Budget options can sometimes be surprisingly agreeable, sometimes a decision to regret.

As the Chinese take to the road as tourists and business travellers, the supply of mid-range hotel options is increasing, in turn decreasing prices and improving quality. There are now even chains of lower mid-range to budget hotels with perfectly acceptable accommodation (without restaurant facilities) such as the Home Inn or Motel 168 chains. Remember, however, that these chains target Chinese travellers, so get ready with your phrase book, and expect to be in a less than central location.

The Dunhuang Hotel on the Silk Road

Modern yurt near Hohhot, Inner Mongolia

As supply increases, advance reservations are becoming less of a necessity except at peak periods. Book in advance for the Spring Festival in late January and for the two great Chinese holiday breaks, the first weeks of May and October, when not only are hotels (except the top tier) fully booked, they are also legally permitted by the government to increase their rates by 50 per cent. Of course, it is reassuring to have a room booked when arriving in a strange city abroad. Plenty of internet-based travel agencies (*www.travelchinaguide.com*; *www.sinohotels.com*) offer this service, sometimes with comments from previous guests. Check the location of the hotel carefully – Chinese cities are always surrounded by large suburbs far from the attractions you've come to see.

If you arrive without a reservation, take no notice of the posted rates – discounts are almost always available, ranging from 30 to 50 per cent. At mid-range and below level hotels, it's a good idea to see the room before registering. You will be asked to show your passport and pay a deposit – often for the full amount of your stay – plus a security deposit. Be sure to keep your receipt. Not all hotels of the mid-range and below categories will accept credit cards – you should enquire in advance. Check-out time is invariably at noon, and half-day rates are charged if you wish to stay even a few hours longer.

Internet facilities are available in all hotels of mid-range level and above. Most rooms in China will be supplied with tea sachets, bottled water and a kettle. Tap water is not generally safe for drinking. Mid-range level hotels and above will also have a mini-bar with soft drinks and beer. Be sure that anything you plug into an electric

Traditional red brightens the Bamboo Garden Hotel in Beijing

socket is 220V, 50 cycles AC, and in any case bring an electric plug adaptor – Chinese sockets are a mixture of many standards, two and three pin, round and flat.

Hotel fires occur too frequently in China – smoke alarms are not common, but heavy drinking and smoking are. Check for fire exits on your floor.

Single male guests will often receive telephone calls proposing massages – those foolish enough to accept this solicitation could find themselves victims of robbery or worse. If this happens once, unplug your telephone until morning, or telephone the reception telling them to block calls to your room. Thefts by hotel staff are extremely rare in China, but take common sense precautions, such as putting any valuables in a locked suitcase, or if the hotel has an in-room safe, use it.

While standards of cleanliness and efficiency are improving, the main complaint foreigners have these days with Chinese hotels is that they are modern and without character. Some small inns are to be found in the *hutongs* of Beijing, and a few colonial buildings in Qingdao and Tianjin have been converted into hotels, but those seeking accommodation in traditional-style Chinese buildings will need to look long and hard. In small towns and villages, home stays are starting to blossom. While the experience will no doubt be interesting, expect to live like the locals. Camping is possible, but only as part of an organised tour specialising in these activities. You can stay at pilgrims' inns at religious sites, such as the sacred Taoist or Buddhist mountains, but again, prepare for a spartan experience.

Star ratings

The Chinese government's mandated star rating system is a good, but not absolutely uniform, guide. Stars are awarded mostly on service quality, facilities and hygiene, but political connections can influence allocation. Ratings of 1 to 3 stars are awarded by provincial authorities, with 3 stars having to be approved by the national tourism administration. Ratings of 4 and 5 stars can only be awarded by the national authority. Be especially careful at the 5-star level – this is where local connections can come into play.

The newer international wing of the Chini Bagh hotel, Kashgar, offers luxury accommodation

With few exceptions, only the international chains have the facilities that qualify them to be considered true 5-star hotels.

No stars

While much depends on the attitude of staff, the quality in such establishments is usually disappointing. Sometimes the proprietors know this from past experience with foreign guests and you will be told that the hotel is full even if it is not.

1 star

Simple, but with air conditioning, sometimes a coffee shop and a majority of rooms with private bath.

2 stars

Air conditioned, most rooms with private bath, offering Chinese food.

3 stars

Fully decorated and well-equipped rooms, elevators, IDD telephones in rooms, television, in-house movies, 24-hour running hot and cold water.

4 stars

Deluxe, fully equipped rooms with extras such as hairdryers, business centre, fitness centre, swimming pool, medical centre and a range of restaurants and bars.

5 stars

Standards that match the very best in the world.

Food and drink

The Chinese love to eat not only for sustenance and taste, but for the social aspect of communal dining. A common greeting, 'Chi fan le mei you?' *literally means 'Have you eaten yet?' While not all Chinese are gourmets, it is rare to find one that does not enjoy food. They can do so with a clear conscience and on the very best of authorities – Confucius himself pointed out that 'eating is the first happiness'.*

Beijing offers arguably the best culinary experiences in China. It's definitely not as glitzy as Shanghai because it favours substance over form, but in terms of the range of serious options, it is hard to find better food in China.

Of course there is the famous Beijing duck, but choices go much further. All of the regional cuisines of China, from delicate Cantonese to spicy Sichuan, are here as well as other Asian cuisines, notably Thai, Indian and Japanese.

Those hungry for a taste of home need not simply patronise the hotel coffee shop because European restaurants are also popular with the locals. Steakhouses and Italian restaurants are the most numerous, although French and even Russian restaurants are found here. Fast food chains such as McDonald's and KFC are hard to miss, and the more upscale American chains, such as TGI Fridays and Tony Roma's, also have a presence in Beijing.

Chinese food is always served in communal style, that is, the host orders several (sometimes too many) dishes which are placed on a revolving platform in the middle of the table and shared by all. You will be served an individual bowl of rice upon which to place the pieces you take from the communal serving plates. Chinese

Chinese cooking is a delicate, refined art

Food sold from street kitchens is cheap and delicious, and is usually freshly prepared while you wait

dining etiquette is rather unrestrained, with slurping of soup definitely permitted and bones left on the table.

The Chinese are painfully aware that foreigners are not interested in their more esoteric specialities such as snake and dog, so you need not worry about such surprises. Tipping is not expected in Chinese restaurants, although the upscale places and the foreign chains will add a service charge of 15 per cent to the bill. Credit cards are accepted in mid-range to upscale restaurants.

CHOPSTICKS

Chopsticks can be awkward to master at first. Perseverance is needed to get the technique right, but a Chinese meal is best enjoyed with them, and the two sticks can be surprisingly agile in practised hands. The bottom stick is the 'anvil', held firmly between the first joint of the ring finger and the lower thumb, while resting in the crook of forefinger and thumb. The top stick is held like a pen between the tip of the thumb and forefinger, and pivots against the lower stick. Practice makes perfect!

Beijing cuisine

The signature dish of the capital is of course Beijing duck, which all must try when they visit the city. Famous restaurants specialise in serving only this dish. The recipe requires a special type of duck, an elaborate method of preparation, and cooking in a special type of oven, all necessary to assure that the skin is both crispy and succulent. The skin and meat of the roasted duck are cut thinly and eaten in pancakes along with spring onions, cucumber and sweet plum sauce. The meal ends with a soup made from the duck's carcass. As the north relies on wheat for its staple food, bread and noodles are more common than rice in Beijing cuisine, and steamed dumplings, called *jiaozi*, make a good quick lunch.

As good as Chinese food is, sometimes it's nice to pick up a fork for a taste of home, and you won't be disappointed here. Beijing has many good Western-style restaurants, from Italian pastas to American steaks and French *haute cuisine*. Vegetarians may have to search harder – vegetarianism in China is practised for spiritual not health reasons. The best bet for finding vegetarian fare is around Buddhist temples.

Since all regional cuisines are available in Beijing and other cities of North China, it is worth noting them here.

Cantonese cuisine

Guangdong Province, source of Cantonese cuisine, is an extremely fertile area, yielding several harvests annually and with a long coastline that provides an abundance of seafood. These fresh ingredients are mostly steamed or stir-fried, ensuring that their flavours and textures are retained. Consequently, they need little support in the way of spices or sauces, although light sauces of garlic, ginger and spring onions are favoured.

Sichuan cuisine

Spice is the variety of life in Sichuan, and the fiery taste of the province's cuisine, laced with red-hot peppers, is renowned throughout China. The pepper varieties in Sichuan give food a sharp, lemony taste, different from the standard chilli flavour. Although hot and spicy is the basic approach, the cuisine offers much more, and chefs

Mung bean noodles from Beijing

work with a medley of seven tastes – sweet, sour, salty, fragrant, bitter, nutty and hot – to achieve a balanced effect. Sichuan's subtlety is present in tea-smoked and camphor-smoked duck, while tangerine-peel chicken and pork with vegetables and bamboo shoots in a sweet sauce are delicately flavoured dishes.

Other styles

In Muslim restaurants and households, particularly in the far west, mutton takes the place of pork and pilaf rice is used in place of plain boiled rice. Uighur food in Xinjiang, apart from the ubiquitous use of mutton, features a variety of dairy products, including some of the best yoghurt in the world, and plenty of bread. Kebabs can be found on just about every street corner, and in any tiny oasis, throughout the province. Hunan likes its spices, but uses them in a more restrained way than Sichuan. Few dishes enjoy the exotic reputation of the Mongolian hotpot. This helps the northerners survive their long and harsh winters, and is in fact a kind of soup in which vegetables and meat are first cooked in boiling water at the table, and then eaten; the bouillon gradually becomes more flavourful and is drunk at the meal's end.

Beverages

Tea is the most popular drink in China, but other beverages, some far less benign, are enjoyed. Sweet wines and liqueurs made from fruits, flowers or herbs can be tasteful and sometimes potent drinks. Western-style wines are now produced in several regions of China. In Beijing, brands such as Great Wall and Dynasty are well known and, while not world class, are quite drinkable. Beware of *mao tai*, the most famous of Chinese clear liquors used in the *gan bei* (bottoms up) toast at banquets. Chinese beer, especially the light and fragrant lager-style Tsingtao (which is still brewed according to a 1900s German recipe), is of a high standard and is extremely refreshing with spicy foods.

Steaming rolls the Sichuan way

Entertainment

Shanghai may beat Beijing as the most culturally avant-garde city in China, but Beijing arguably still retains the top position for those seeking more classical and less raucous forms of entertainment. Musical performances (both Chinese and by the best touring troupes from abroad), dance, opera and acrobatics are all of a high standard here.

There's plenty of participatory entertainment as well, from quiet cafés and pubs beside the lakes to laser-show discos and jazz clubs. Outside Bejing, the options are limited, especially if you're not fond of karaoke. The best sources of information on both upcoming performances and the hippest new nightspots are the English language entertainment magazines *City Weekend* or *That's Bejing*. These are distributed free in hotels and restaurants, and both have websites: *www.cityweekend.com.cn* and *www.thatsbj.com.*

Harbin beer at a Harbin street café

The performing arts

A visit to a Beijing opera (*see pp32–3*) is almost obligatory for visitors to the city. Yes, it's cacophonous, and no, you won't understand the dialogue, but most people come away with the feeling of having experienced something unique and extraordinary. There are now some venues that offer shortened versions and programmes in English, but they are obviously not the real thing. If you have the time and interest, try to seek out a traditional performance.

Chinese acrobats, like their gymnasts, enjoy worldwide acclaim. High-wire balancing acts, plate-spinning, human pyramids and the like need no translation and make for an amusing evening for the whole family. While Shanghai is traditionally the most famous venue for acrobatic performances, Beijing has its own acrobatics troupe which gives regular performances.

Classical music performances, both Western and Chinese, are another option for those seeking higher culture in their entertainment. Beijing is justifiably proud of its Beijing Symphony Orchestra, and foreign orchestras often perform in the capital. The usual venue for such performances is the **Beijing Yinyue Ting (Beijing Concert Hall)** (*1 Beixinhua Jie. Tel: (010) 6835 1383*) although the new **National Theatre**, the immense dome-like structure on Chang'an Jie just west of Tiananmen Square, will gradually take over for the most important events.

Traditional musical recitals are still very popular

The club scene

Those seeking live musical performances of a more modern nature will find a good range of choices in Beijing. Rock, jazz and hip-hop venues abound, some of them quite good, some atrocious. Jazz speaks the universal language of melody, and there are some good jazz clubs in town, usually more sedate than the rock-oriented venues. The San Li Tun Bar Street and the Chaoyang Park area are the main music areas, but again, check the entertainment magazines for the current acts performing.

Stylish dance clubs are favoured by the well-off young Beijingers and expatriates. The latest mixes played by DJs who know the craft, English menus and attentive staff characterise these clubs. Cover charges can exceed 100 RMB to keep out the proletariat, but single men should be warned that some of the sweet young ladies smiling across the bar may well be practitioners of the world's oldest profession.

Bars and pubs

If you feel like an evening drink without loud music or dancing, Beijing can oblige. The busiest watering holes are found cheek by jowl with the clubs

The new National Theatre at night

of San Li Tun Bar Street and are only differentiated by the lack of loud music. Mainly active on weekends, they cater mostly to Chinese and a few expats. The bars of Chaoyang Garden are a little less wild, but you are most likely to find something to your liking in the area around the Back Lakes of Shicha Hai or Hou Hai. Theme bars are becoming popular, with everything from American Wild West saloons to British pubs competing for the drinker's time and money.

Cafés and teahouses

If it's not intoxication you seek, the cafés and teahouses of Beijing are your best choice for people-watching and whiling away the day or evening. Outside Beijing, traditional teahouses are really all you can hope to find, but they're more atmospheric in any case. The Starbucks chain has hit Beijing with a vengeance (including a branch within the Forbidden City that was evicted after protests by locals), but there are many locally owned cafés that offer more for less. Light food is served in most cafés, although usually not in teahouses. The best place to have a tea or coffee in Beijing is alongside one of the lakes or in the university district of Haidian.

A few teahouses offer entertainment in the form of Beijing opera, magic performances, comedy shows and acrobatics. Particularly good is the **Lao She Teahouse** (*3rd floor, Da Wan Cha Building, 3 Qianmen Xu. Tel: (010) 6303 6830. Performances: 7.40pm–9.20pm. Admission charge*) named after one of China's most famous 20th century novelists and dramatists (his most famous play *Cha Guan* is set in a teahouse).

Art galleries

Throughout China's history, painting and calligraphy have been highly respected arts in court and intellectual circles. They were usually produced by scholars and mandarins who had artistic training and plenty of leisure time to produce the high-quality brushwork necessary for painting and calligraphy. Today, these arts are shared by many ordinary people and Beijing's art galleries attest to this fact. The city is home to a host of fine galleries and exhibitions change regularly. For a contemporary look at Chinese art try **Art Scene Beijing** (*798-Dashanzi, 2 Jiu Xianqiao, Chaoyang District. Tel: (010) 6431 6962. www.artscenebeijing.com. Open: 10am–6pm*). The **Red Gate Gallery** (*Levels 1 and 4, Dongbianmen Watchtower, Chongwenmen. Tel: (010) 6525 1005. www.redgategallery.com. Open: 10am–5pm*) showcases a number of China's very best contemporary artists. For a more traditional approach the **Wan Fung Art Gallery** (*136 Nanchizi, Dongcheng District. Tel: (010) 6523 3320. www.wanfung.com.cn. Open: 10am–6pm*) promotes contemporary masters working within long-established media.

Cinema

Since the Chinese government bans or censors both foreign and (particularly) Chinese films, the fare in most cinemas is limited – some Chinese circumvent this by buying pirated DVDs, or downloading films from the internet. Outside Beijing, if you want to relax with a movie, you'd best do it in your hotel room – almost all are equipped with DVD players.

A performance of Chinese opera at Liyuan Theatre in Beijing

Shopping

China manages to combine a great variety of styles, price ranges and standards in its shopping. By itself this is not so unusual, but the sheer range of shops, stalls and markets that it takes to serve its vast population is awesome. Visitors and locals are likely to have different interests in what they are looking to buy, but markets are definitely one of the best places to see the real China.

The Chinese are great shoppers and even greater bargainers. More importantly, the participants are focused on their shopping, not looking at you, so it's much easier to feel like the observer rather than the observed. If you want to join the game, it's essential to be prepared to bargain, unless you visit only modern shopping malls. Bargaining doesn't come easily to most Westerners, but it can be learned, and in fact is half the fun of shopping. A few tips: If you're in a big market, such as Beijing's Panjiuyuan, you'll quickly notice that many of the shops sell identical items. Ask the price of your object of desire at a few shops to get a rough idea of the asking price. The price will often be shown to you on a calculator, which is then handed to you to make a counter-offer. Start with 25 per cent of the asking price, which will probably be refused, so just smile and leave, but don't be surprised if you're called back. Above all, keep smiling. While Beijing is certainly the best place for shopping in Northern China, Xian and other cities have interesting markets. Almost every city has a *hua niao shichang* (bird and flower market) where local crafts are also sold. In Beijing, besides Panjiuyuan (also known as the Ghost Market or the Dirt Market), which is a bit distant,

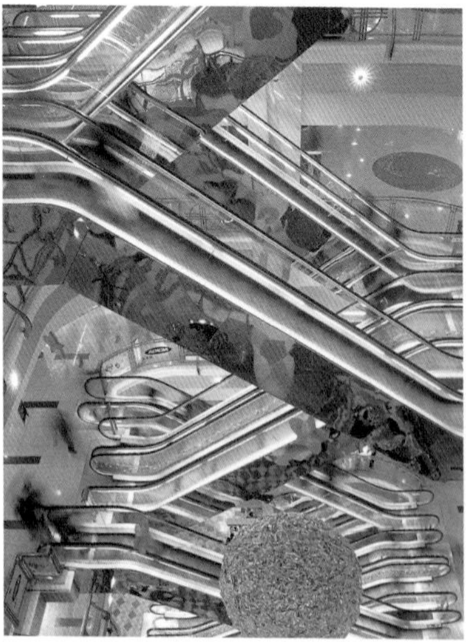

The glittering mall has made an appearance in China as well

Whether you buy or not, souvenir hunting in the Panjiayuan market in Beijing is enjoyable

another popular shopping area for visitors is Liulichang, southwest of Qianmen at the southern end of Tiananmen Square.

For those not interested in the hustle and bustle of the market, the upscale malls of Wangfujing Dajie are worth seeing. This is a pedestrian-only zone within walking distance of the Forbidden City. Here you'll find both Western luxury goods and dozens of smaller boutiques selling locally produced clothing as well as souvenirs. Much of the world's clothing is now produced in China, including top brands of sportswear, but the real thing is no cheaper here than at home, so buy only what you might need for your trip.

Counterfeiting is big business in China. 'Designer clothes', 'antiques' and 'antiquities' are mass produced in supposedly illegal factories (the Chinese authorities have done little to stamp them out). Remember that counterfeit goods, be they DVDs or clothing, are likely to be seized by customs authorities when you return home, and you could be subject to a fine as well.

Antiques – items not more than 180 years old, stamped with an official wax seal – should be what they purport to be; those from street markets are extremely unlikely to be to genuine. Anything more than 180 years old is classed as an antiquity and cannot be exported, although occasionally you will be approached by people offering them – don't even think about it. Another potential problem is the 'art student' scam, where a smiling young Chinese will suggest you go together to see great bargains at a special gallery he knows. Smile and depart, or you will be cheated. Despite all these caveats, there are plenty of fine products and souvenirs that you can bring back from China.

Sport and leisure

Beijing is not really a sportsperson's paradise, largely due to the weather and pollution, but outside the city those seeking serious exercise will find plenty to do. Hiking and cycling opportunities abound near the Ming Tombs and in Chengde. Further afield, foregoing the cable cars and climbing the well-laid pilgrim paths and staircases on any of the sacred mountains is certainly good exercise.

Along the coast, swimming and sailing are possible when weather permits. The 2008 Olympics have left in their wake some superb sporting venues, which are now sometimes open to the public.

The Chinese have their own sporting traditions, largely in the martial arts and the softer permutations of it. Wushu, more commonly known as kung fu in the West, belongs to a tradition stretching back thousands of years. Chinese wrestling, tai chi (*see box*) and qigong (a fitness exercise aimed at controlling the mind and regulating breathing to improve overall health and physiology) are other examples of traditional Chinese sport. Courses in English can be arranged by fitness centres in hotels.

Participatory sports

All of the top hotels in Beijing and the other major cities in Northern China have fitness centres, a swimming pool and tennis courts. Some have evolved into spas and offer massage and other therapeutic treatments. Non-residents can often use the facilities by paying an entrance fee or by becoming a member of the hotel's club. Golf in China is an extension of the boardroom, where

Tai chi

Paragliding over the Great Wall

deals are sealed between shots. Given the shortage of water in Northern China, it's not the most eco-friendly pursuit, but if you're in need of a game, the most favourably situated course is that of the Beijing International Golf Club (*see p163*). Bowling is a well-loved indoor sport, with hundreds of bowling alleys from deluxe to run-down found in all major cities. Both indoor and outdoor ice skating are popular in the winter. Kite flying is a fun and relaxing way to spend an afternoon, and is enjoyed on Tiananmen Square or any big public square throughout China.

Spectator sports

The 2008 Olympics have increased China's passion for spectator sports, and regular competitions are held. Beijingers love their local football team, called Guo An, which has recruited some foreign players. The Beijing Ducks, the local basketball team, play during the winter.

Check the entertainment magazines for scheduled events.

TAI CHI

Called *taijiquan* in Chinese, it is better known as tai chi in the West. Tai chi consists of a set of movements designed to exercise the body and mind. The aim is for the mind to control the movements of the body, which are graceful and gentle but complex. Many Chinese begin their day with a tai chi session in a park or in the street, and there is a restful, almost mesmerising, quality to the sight of hundreds of people moving to the natural rhythm of this exercise, which was formalised in the 17th century. People all over the world practise tai chi, and if you have a modicum of skill, you're welcome to join any group practising in China.

Children

China is not the easiest place to travel with children, and perhaps should not be the first overseas destination to accustom your kids to the joys of travel. The long travelling times, the lack of attractions for children, and the unfamiliarity of the food can make this a challenge for families.

There are some specialist travel agencies that organise escorted tours especially for families with children, emphasising natural rather than cultural attractions. For tours covering all of China, try *www.imperialtours.net*; for Beijing day tours with kid-focused itineraries, try *www.tour-beijing.com*. If you're determined to show China to your children, this is your best choice.

Beijing is certainly an easier place for families with young children than elsewhere in China, and the further you get off the beaten track, the more challenging it becomes. All the baby formula, disposable nappies and other assorted paraphernalia of the West are found in Beijing and major cities. In Beijing there are some attractions that will please children, such as the Beijing Aquarium (*see p161*) and the **China Puppet Theatre** (*Zhongguo Muou Juyuan, 1 Anhua Shi Li, Beisanhuan. Tel: (010) 6422 9487*). Kite flying or a trip to an ice skating rink are good options as well. In the Oriental Plaza mall, the **Sony Explora-Science Centre** (*1 Wangfujing Dajie. Tel: (010) 8518 2255. Open: 10am–6pm. Admission charge*) has great interactive exhibits aimed at children. Chinese zoos, however, with their bars and cages, are usually depressing for adults and frightening for children brought up

ONE-CHILD FAMILIES

Faced with the need to slow down the growth in China's population, the government adopted a 'one child per family' policy (national minorities are exempt). Large families are traditionally seen as a source of security for parents' old age, and this policy meant a traumatic change in lifestyle. Boys are preferred, and through ultrasound tests followed by abortion of female foetuses, the male/female ratio has been upset, with ten boys for every eight girls born. Ironically, China is also worried that pampered single children, or 'little emperors' as they are called, are growing up as a spoiled generation. Spoiled they may be, but in urban areas they are also stressed because the family's expectations are channelled to the single child, who studies hours longer than in the West.

with any conception of animal rights. Outside Beijing, the choices reduce dramatically.

Children under 1.1m (3½ft) get half-price admission at attractions, but that's about the only accommodation made for them. Restaurants rarely have high chairs suitable for young children, and if you're travelling with a stroller, you'll quickly notice that the pavements are irregular and escalators only run up.

The Chinese are quite demonstrative about their affection for children, including those of strangers. A blonde-haired blue-eyed toddler can be the source of so much attention as to make children (and their parents) a little uncomfortable. It's not unheard of to have your child scooped up and hugged by complete strangers, and requests for photo opportunities can seem to never end. Although the intention is good, it can get tiring quickly. On the other hand, the Chinese are likely to make special efforts to please families with children in hotels and restaurants.

Children will enjoy flying unusual kites

Essentials

Arriving and departing

By air

Beijing's Capital Airport was renovated and a terminal added for the 2008 Olympics. It is connected to the city by a light rail system.
Tel: (010) 6454 1100).
http://en.bcia.com.cn

Airport tax

Airport taxes are included in the price of air tickets when they are purchased.

By road

It is possible to enter China by bus or on foot from Kazakhstan, Kyrgyzstan, Laos, Mongolia, Nepal, Pakistan, Russia and Vietnam.

By rail

Most people travelling by train in China use the Hong Kong–Guangzhou Express. More exotic routes, such as the Trans-Siberian Express, are also popular, while a new route from Kazakhstan to Xinjiang has recently opened.

Customs

The duty-free limits are 2 litres of alcohol, 600 cigarettes and 0.5 litres of perfume. There is a notional limit of 1,000 minutes of video film and 72 rolls of still film. Unlimited amounts of foreign currency can be imported, but amounts above US$10,000 need to be declared and foreign exchange receipts retained if the balance is to be re-exported at the end of your trip. Chinese customs are strict with illegal narcotics and pornographic or anti-government literature. Excessive amounts of religious literature also cause grounds for suspicion.

Electricity

The electricity supply is 220 volts, 50 cycles AC. Several socket types are in use for which a multiple adaptor plug should be purchased before departure.

Internet

While most hotels have internet facilities, private internet cafés can be grim dens filled with chain-smoking teenagers playing online games. If you have a laptop, wi-fi is commonly found in Beijing's hipper cafés.

Money

The main unit of currency is the yuan (¥) or renminbi (RMB), meaning 'the people's money'. Yuan and RMB are interchangeable. The yuan is divided into 10 jiao, and one jiao is divided into 10 fen. Notes are issued in denominations of 100, 50, 10, 5, 2 and 1 yuan, and 5, 2 and 1 jiao. Coins are 1 yuan, and 5, 2 and 1 jiao.

Credit cards, traveller's cheques, ATMs

Credit cards are accepted in good restaurants, hotels and large tourist outlets. US dollars, euros and British pounds can be changed in banks and hotels. The exchange rates are centrally fixed, and there is no 'black market' for currency. The easiest way to obtain Chinese cash is by using your credit card in a local ATM (cash machine). Bank of China ATMs always accept foreign credit cards. Debit cards are less reliable, and bank-issued credit cards usually don't work.

Opening hours

Government offices and public institutions open from 8am or 9am until 5pm or 6pm, with a two-hour break at lunch. Sunday is usually the weekly closing day, although some banks and foreign exchange offices may open on Sunday morning. Big department stores open daily 9am–7pm. Private businesses, such as shops and restaurants, open from early in the morning until late in the evening, and even into the early hours of the morning.

Passports and visas

All visitors to China must obtain a visa before arrival, issued by Chinese embassies and consulates. They can be obtained at short notice from the travel agencies in Hong Kong and Macao. Rules are becoming less stringent, with three-month and multiple-entry visitor visas available, extendable by application to the Public Security Bureau in China. Overstaying guarantees a fine of 100 RMB per day and delays at the airport.

Pharmacies

Because many Western medicines are not available in China, you should take your own prescription drugs and a supply of minor medicaments when you travel. The same applies to tampons, contraceptives and nappies.

Post office at the Summer Palace, Beijing

There is always a 24-hour pharmacy in big cities. For more serious problems, ask your hotel or guide for assistance. In Beijing, diplomatic missions have their own medical arrangements and usually offer advice to foreigners.

Post

Main post offices are open 8am–6pm and offer a wide range of postal services. Like many government-operated bodies in China, however, the postal service is overstaffed and inefficient.

Public holidays

1 January	New Year
Late January/ early February	Chinese New Year (2/3-day holiday)
8 March	Women's Day
1 May	Labour Day
4 May	Youth Day
1 June	Children's Day
1 July	Communist Party Day
1 August	People's Liberation Army Day
1 October	National Day

Smoking

Smoking is socially acceptable almost anywhere. Some long-distance air-conditioned buses do try to stop smoking on board, often with little success. Airports are also supposed to be smoke-free, but rarely is this enforced.

Suggested reading and media

All major foreign newspapers and magazines are available in Beijing. The English-language newspaper the *China Daily* is mainly filled with favourable 'news' about how well China is solving its problems. English-language entertainment publications are available free in some big cities. They are available in bars, restaurants and hotels in Beijing. Titles include: *Beijing City Weekend* and *That's Beijing*.

Sustainable tourism

Thomas Cook is a strong advocate of ethical and fairly traded tourism and believes that the travel experience should be as good for the places visited as it is for the people who visit them. That's why we firmly support The Travel Foundation, a charity that develops solutions to help improve and protect holiday destinations, their environment, traditions and culture. To find out what you can do to make a positive difference to the places you travel to and the people who live there, please visit *www.thetravelfoundation.org.uk*

Tax

Top end hotels usually, but by no means always, levy a 15 per cent service charge.

Telephones

Calling home from China

UK and Northern Ireland: *00* + *44* + area code (without first *0*)
Republic of Ireland: *00* + *353* + area code (without first *0*)
USA and Canada: *00* + *1* + area code
Australia: *00* + *61* + area code
New Zealand: *00* + *64* + area code
South Africa: *00* + *27* + area code

Calling China from abroad

To call China from abroad, dial the access code *00* from the UK, Ireland and New Zealand; *011* from the USA and Canada; *0011* from Australia, followed by the country code for China, *86* and the regional number without the first *0* in the area code.

CONVERSION TABLE

FROM	TO	MULTIPLY BY
Inches	Centimetres	2.54
Feet	Metres	0.3048
Yards	Metres	0.9144
Miles	Kilometres	1.6090
Acres	Hectares	0.4047
Gallons	Litres	4.5460
Ounces	Grams	28.35
Pounds	Grams	453.6
Pounds	Kilograms	0.4536
Tons	Tonnes	1.0160

To convert back, for example from centimetres to inches, divide by the number in the third column.

Mobile phones

China uses the European GSM mobile telephone system, although the US CDMA system is making inroads. You can either bring your own phone or buy an inexpensive one in China for your trip – just insert an easily bought prepaid SIM card. If you're travelling throughout China, make sure your SIM card is valid in all provinces – the cheapest ones are valid within a certain city or province only.

Time zone

All of China uses Beijing's time zone, which makes for dark mornings in the far west. The capital's time is Greenwich Mean Time (GMT) + 8 hours, and Eastern Daylight Time (EDT) + 13 hours. This puts Beijing 8 hours ahead of London, 13 hours ahead of New York and 2 hours behind Melbourne.

Toilets

Except in tourist areas, public toilets are not very pleasant, and squatting in public over an open sluice is fairly common. It is wise to take your own toilet paper or tissues. Toilets in the bigger hotels and restaurants are usually good, and the squeamish would be well advised to wait for such opportunities.

Travellers with disabilities

Lack of facilities, difficulty of access and overloaded transport make life hard for those with mobility problems. For further information, contact:

UK

Royal Association for Disability and Rehabilitation (RADAR)
12 City Forum, 250 City Road
London EC1V 8AF.
Tel: (020) 7250 3222.

USA

Society for Accessible Travel & Hospitality
347 Fifth Avenue, Suite 610
New York, NY 10016.
Tel: (212) 447 7284.

Language

China's principal language is Mandarin, a term that originates from the Portuguese word *mandar* (to govern), and the language was previously used in connection with imperial officials who spoke their own 'official language'.

The Beijing variant of Mandarin (minus the capital's characteristic 'burr') is the official language of the country and is called *putonghua* (common speech). Both Mandarin and the dialects use tones integral to the correct pronunciation of the word, adding to the difficulty for foreigners.

The pinyin system of romanising Chinese can be both helpful and confusing, but it is fairly widely used. It is useful to know the pinyin name for a destination you may be trying to find; for example, you are likely to find your way better if you ask not for the Great Hall of the People, but the Renmin Dahui Tang. Some pronunciation hints:

PRONUNCIATION

c	ts as in cats
q	ch
x	sh
z	dz as in kids
zh	j

TRANSPORT

airplane	fei ji
airport	fei ji chang
bus	gong gong qi che
bus station	gong gong qi che zhan
train	huo che
railway station	huo che zhan
car	qi che
taxi	chu zu qi che
bicycle	xi xing che

NUMBERS

1	yi
2	er
3	san
4	si
5	wu
6	liu
7	qi
8	ba
9	jiu
10	shi
20	ershi
30	sanshi
40	sishi
50	wushi
100	yibai
1,000	yiqian

FOOD AND DRINK

rice	fan
fried rice	chao fan
noodles	mian tiao
egg	ji dan
fish	yu
duck	ya zi
chicken	ji
beef	niu rou
pork	zhu rou
shrimp	xia mi
soup	tang
bread	mianbao
fruit	guo zi
plain water	kai shui
tea	cha
coffee	ka fei

WEEKDAYS

Monday	xing qi yi
Tuesday	xing qi er
Wednesday	xing qi san
Thursday	xing qi si
Friday	xing qi wu
Saturday	xing qi liu
Sunday	xing qi tian

ACCOMMODATION

Hotel	Fan dian
Guesthouse	Bing guan
Do you have a room?	Ni you bu you fang jian?
How much is it?	Duo shao qian?
Toilet	Ce suo

GENERAL PHRASES

Hello	Ni hao
Goodbye	Zai jian
How are you?	Ni hao ma?
Thank you	Xie xie ni
Please	Qing
Excuse me	Lao jia
I am sorry	Duibuqi
When?	Shen me shi hou?
What is this?	Zhei shi shen mo?
I understand	Wo dong
I don't understand	Wo bu dong
Do you understand?	Ni dong bu dong?
Yes	Shi
No	Bu shi
I like...	Wo xihuan …
I don't like...	Wo bu xihuan …
How much is this?	Zhei shi duo shao qian?
Too expensive	Tai gui
Inexpensive	Bu gui pian yi
I would like to go to …	Wo yao qu …
Where is the …?	Zai nar …?
I would like a ticket	Wo yao mai piao
Straight ahead	Yi zhi zou
Left	Zuo bian
Right	You bian
Today	Jin tian
Yesterday	Ming tian
Tomorrow	Zuo tian

Emergencies

Emergency telephone numbers

Accidents/ambulance: *120*
Police: *110*
Fire: *119*

Medical services

Casualty

Medical treatment for foreigners in China is not free and can sometimes be expensive. Before receiving treatment at any hospital you should try to contact your insurers to make sure that you are fully covered. Ensure that your travel insurance documents are with you at all times – hospitals will need to see these before dispensing any treatment.

If you fall ill outside of Beijing, it should be handled through a hotel concierge or tour leader.

Doctors

China has some of the best doctors in the world pursuing both Chinese traditional medicine and Western practices. Most major cities will have private hospitals and clinics with English-speaking doctors. Many of these private institutions have been set up by foreign companies. Some of the larger pharmacies have a doctor on their staff.

Opticians

In the larger cities there are some excellent opticians, many of whom speak English. Prescription lenses with fashionable frames are available at prices well below what you would find in the West. Cheap reading glasses are available in many shops.

Health and insurance

It is recommended that travellers keep tetanus and polio vaccinations up to date, and be vaccinated against typhoid and hepatitis A. Precautions against malaria should be taken by those travelling to rural areas or making river trips. Observe food and water hygiene precautions: drink bottled water, and ensure that food is cleanly prepared.

Be sure to take out comprehensive travel insurance before you travel to China.

Safety and crime

Overall, tourists are unlikely to be affected by violent crime in China. More common are scams designed to separate you from your money, usually practised by touts pretending to be students. While the Chinese are friendly towards foreigners (and like to practise their English) and you need not isolate yourself from such harmless contacts, do not allow yourself to be taken to buy anything, or go to a restaurant or bar with anyone you meet on the street. This is a standard *modus operandi* of con artists, and your new friend might leave you with a grossly inflated bill to pay.

Pickpocketing and bag slicing occurs, but can be avoided with a few sensible precautions such as carrying only the money you need with you in a front trouser pocket. Make a photocopy of your passport, including the page with your Chinese visa, and leave the original in your hotel with other valuables. Be especially careful in markets and train stations. City streets are safe and relaxed at night.

Prostitution, although illegal, flourishes in the big cities, and carries the same inherent dangers as anywhere.

Lost property
Airports, railway stations and the more important bus depots all have lost property offices. You should report loss of goods to the police.

Embassies

Foreign embassies in Beijing include:

Australia
21 Dongzhimenwai.
Tel: (010) 6532 2331.

Canada
19 Dongzhimenwai.
Tel: (010) 6532 3536.

Ireland
3 Ritan Dong.
Tel: (010) 6532 2691/2914.

New Zealand
1 Ritan Dong.
Tel: (010) 6532 2731/3.

UK
11 Guanghua.
Tel: (010) 6532 1961.

USA
3 Xiushui Bei.
Tel: (010) 6532 3831.

Chinese embassies abroad:

Australia
15 Coronation Drive, Yarralumla, Canberra.
Tel: (02) 6273 4783.

Canada
515 St Patrick Street, Ottawa, Ontario, K1N 5H3.
Tel: (613) 789 3434.

Ireland
40 Ailesbury Road, Dublin 4.
Tel: (1) 269 1707.

New Zealand
2–6 Glenmore Street, Kelburn, Wellington.
Tel: (04) 472 1382.

UK
49–51 Portland Place, London W1B 1JL.
Tel: (020) 7299 8428.

USA
2300 Connecticut Avenue NW, Washington, DC 20008.
Tel: (202) 328 2500.

Police

The police are known as the Public Security Bureau (PSB), and officers wear green uniforms with peaked caps, not dissimilar to the uniforms of the PLA (People's Liberation Army). They are generally, though not always, helpful to foreigners, but this may be made difficult by the language barrier. The Foreign Affairs Branch of the local PSB deals with foreigners, and is staffed with officials who speak English.

Directory

Accommodation price guide

The accommodation prices are based on the cost per person for two people sharing the least expensive double room with an en suite bathroom and including breakfast.

★	Under 500 RMB
★★	500–1,000 RMB
★★★	1,001–1,500 RMB
★★★★	Above 1,500 RMB

Eating out price guide

Price ranges are per person for a three-course meal without drinks.

★	Under 40 RMB
★★	40–80 RMB
★★★	81–150 RMB
★★★★	Above 150 RMB

BEIJING

ACCOMMODATION

Zhonggong Beijing Shi Wei Ban Jiguan Zhaodaisuo ★
Despite having a mouthful of a name, this government-run hostel is a fine choice for budget accommodation. It has friendly staff and lots going on, including bicycle rental and local tours. *71 Dong Si Liu Tiao, Dongcheng District. Tel: (010) 6401 8823, ext 8100. Fax: (010) 6401 8823, ext 8200. Metro: Beixinqiao.*

Lusong Yuan Binguan ★–★★
Located on the site of a Qing Dynasty general's residence, this charming hotel is built around five courtyards, each decorated delightfully with rockeries and potted plants. The quaint rooms have high ceilings and large windows. The hotel also has an excellent Chinese restaurant and teahouse. *22 Banchang Hutong, Kuan Jie, Dongcheng District. Tel: (010) 6401 1116. Fax: (010) 6403 0418. Metro: Guloudajie.*

Bamboo Garden Hotel ★★
A quiet courtyard hotel located a little over 1km (2/3 mile) north of the Forbidden City. The simple rooms are decorated in Ming and Qing Dynasty styles. Rooms are air conditioned and include TV, wireless internet and a refrigerator. The hotel has a restaurant, teahouse and health spa. *24 Xiaoshiqiao Hutong, Jiugulou, Xicheng District. Tel: (010) 6403 2229. Fax: (010) 6401 2633. Email: travel@bbgh.com.cn. www.bbgh.com.cn. Metro: Guloudajie.*

Hotel Kapok ★★
This is a modern, chic boutique hotel with 89 elegant suites, located close to the Wangfujing shopping area. An excellent Western grill is

available in the evenings.
16 Donghuamen, Dongcheng District. Tel: (010) 6525 9988. Metro: Wangfujing.

Beijing Hotel ★★★
Established in 1900, the Beijing Hotel is the capital's oldest and still remains one of its grandest. Nowadays, this fully modernised hotel has an indoor swimming pool, spa and gymnasium. It is situated a stone's throw from Tiananmen Square.
33 Dongchang'an, Dongcheng District. Tel: (010) 6513 7766. Fax: (010) 6513 7842/ 7703. www. chinabeijinghotel.com. Metro: Wangfujing.

Red Capital Residence ★★★
Named as one of the world's 50 most romantic hotels by *Travel & Leisure* in 2003, this boutique hotel is situated in the preserved heritage district of Beijing. There are only five suites at the Residence, each decorated in an elaborate historical fashion.
9 Dongsi Liutiao, Dongcheng District. Tel: (010) 8403 5308. Fax: (010) 8403 5303. Email: info@redcapitalclub. com.cn. www. redcapitalclub.com.cn. Metro: Zhangzizhonglu.

Peninsula Palace ★★★★
The Peninsula combines Eastern and Western cultures splendidly. The architecture is flamboyantly Chinese and the lobby is decorated with Chinese antiques. The rooms are designed in fine hardwood with authentic rugs and offer all modern amenities.
8 Dongdanbei, Wangfujing, Dongcheng District.Tel: (010) 8516 2888. Fax: (010) 6510 6311. Email: pbi@peninsula.com. www.beijing.peninsula. com. Metro: Dengshikou.

St Regis Hotel ★★★★
Although the most expensive hotel in Beijing, a personal butler is included! Rooms are spacious and luxurious. The hotel is located in the heart of the city's business and shopping district.
21 Jianguomenwai. Tel: (010) 6460 6688. Fax: (010) 6460 3299. www.StRegis.com/Beijing. Metro: Dongzhimen.

EATING OUT

Golden Cat Dumpling City ★
Beijingers love dumplings and there is a choice of no fewer than 30 different fillings at this simple diner, from traditional pork, fish, lamb and beef to pumpkin and aubergine, some spiced with dill, fennel and chives.
East Gate of Tuanjiehu Gongyuan. Tel: (010) 8598 5011. Open: 9am–2am. Metro: Guomao.

Afunti ★★
The capital's largest and best-known Uighur restaurant. The Muslim cuisine – from China's far-flung Xinjiang Province – includes specialities of lamb accompanied by Xinjiang salad and tasty nan bread. Xinjiang dancers and musicians perform nightly at 8pm, followed by audience participation.
2A Houguaibang Hutong, Chaonei. Tel: (010) 6527 2288. Open: Mon–Fri

11am–midnight, Sat & Sun 11am–1am. Metro: Chaoyangmen.

Grandma's Kitchen ★★
A must for homesick Westerners who are craving authentic American meals and atmosphere. It's all here: Philadelphia cheesecake, blueberry pancakes, hamburgers, fries, pizza and more.
11A Xiushui Nam (just south of Ritan Park), Jianguomenwai, Chaoyang District. Tel: (010) 6503 2893. Metro: Yong'anli.

Jinshancheng Chongqing ★★
The largest, and arguably the best, Sichuan restaurant in the capital. This is also one of the most reasonably priced eateries in the city and is always crowded. Try *gongbao jiding* (Sichuan-style diced chicken with chilli peanuts), *ganbian tudou* (a tasty potato dish), *mapou doufu* (spicy tofu) and *laziji* (chicken in hot peppers).
Zhongfu Mansion (2nd floor), 99 Jiangou Lu, Chaoyang District. Tel: (010) 6581 1598. Open: Lunch & dinner. Metro: Guomao.

Lao Hanzi ★★
If you are in the mood for an alternative to Beijing duck and dumplings, sample the cuisine of the Hakka people, originally from Northern China, who now live mainly in Guangdong. Try the tasty *meicai kourou* (fatty pork with preserved vegetables), *sanbei ya* (three cups duck), and *zhuyan xia* (shrimp cooked in rock salt).
Shichahai Dongan (off Sanlitun Bar), Houhai, Dongcheng District. Tel: (010) 6415 3376/ (010) 6404 2259. Open: Lunch & dinner. Metro: Guloudajie.

Li Qun Roast Duck Restaurant ★★
More authentic than the commercial Beijing duck restaurants that most tourists are lured to, this cosy family-run restaurant is hidden down some backstreets in the Qianmen neighbourhood. Delicious, tender duck baked in an authentic oven.
11 Beixiangfeng, Zhengyi, Dongcheng District. Tel: (010) 6705 5578. Open: 11am–11pm. Metro: Chongwenmen.

Fangshan Restaurant ★★★
Beautifully set on the banks of Beihai Lake, this courtyard restaurant serves up imperial dishes once favoured by the Manchu rulers of the Qing Dynasty. Banquet-style meals. Always popular, it's best to book in advance.
1 Wenjing (inside the South Gate of Beihai Gongyuan), Xicheng District. Tel: (010) 6401 1879. Open: Mon–Fri 11am–1.30pm & 5pm–7.30pm, Sat & Sun 10.30am–1.30pm & 4.30pm–8pm. Metro: Tiananmen Xi.

The Courtyard ★★★★
One of Beijing's best-known restaurants, the Courtyard commands a view of the east gate of the Forbidden City. It specialises in exquisite 'Chinese meets Continental' fusion cuisine. Look for treats such as jumbo shrimp with lemongrass-caramel glacé, *foie gras* brûlée, cashew crusted lamb

chops, and sea bass with pickled bell peppers. Excellent selection of wine available.
95 Donghuamen, Dongcheng District. Tel: (010) 6526 8883. Open: 6pm–10pm. Metro: Dengshikou.

Justine's ★★★★
Authentic French cuisine and impeccable service. Favourites include *escargots*, *foie gras* and *Chateaubriand*. Tempting desserts and top French wines available. Also serves an excellent Sunday brunch.
5 Jianguomenwai Dajie, Dongcheng District. Tel: (010) 6500 2233, ext 8039. Metro: Yong'anli.

Red Capital Club ★★★★
Excellent Chinese cuisine served in a beautifully restored courtyard house. Pre-dinner drinks in a bar room crammed with Cultural Revolution memorabilia. The main dining room is decorated with Qing robes and porcelain. The dishes are said to be the favourites of China's top leaders – try Deng's Chicken, Marshal's Delight, lip-searing hot peppers stuffed with pork and shrimp, and a tasty fish baked in a bamboo mat. Reservations essential.
66 Dongsi Jiutiao, Dongcheng District. Tel: 010) 6402 7150. Open: Dinner only. Metro: Zhangzizhonglu.

ENTERTAINMENT

Bai Feng's (No Name Bar)
One of the city's most happening bars, overlooking Lake Houhai. It is outfitted in pot plants, stylish décor and wicker furniture. Ideal spot for an evening cocktail.
3 Qianhai, East Bank, Xicheng District. Tel: (010) 6401 3204. Open: noon–2am. Metro: Guloudajie.

Beijing Dongwuyuan (Beijing Zoo)
A chance to visit China's famous pandas, plus other indigenous animals such as golden monkeys, milu deer and northeast tigers.
Xizhimenwai, Xicheng District. Tel: (010) 6831 4411. Open: 7.30am–5pm. Admission charge. Metro: Xizhimen.

Beijing Yingyue Ting (Beijing Concert Hall) (Classical music and opera)
A principal venue for concerts by both visiting and home-grown orchestras.
Beixinhua. Tel: (010) 6601 8092. Metro: Xidan.

Blue Zoo Beijing (Aquarium)
An underwater aquarium with electric walkway. The 3.5 million litre (770,000-gallon) tank contains thousands of tropical fish.
Worker's Stadium South Gate, Chaoyang District. Tel: (010) 6591 3397. www.blue-zoo.com. Open: Mon–Fri 9.30am–5pm, Sat–Sun 9.30am–6pm. Admission charge. Metro: Chaoyangmen.

Chaoyang Juchang (Chaoyang Theatre) (Acrobatics)
One of the world's premier acrobatic troupes. Performances nightly.
Beijing Chaoyang Theatre, 36 Dongsanhuan Bei, Chaoyang District. Tel: (010) 6507 2421/1818. Daily shows 7.15pm. Metro: Dongzhimen.

Cherry Lane Cinema
A non-profit service that was established to give foreign audiences a chance to see some of China's best contemporary films. Chinese movies with English subtitles are shown most Fridays at 8pm. Directors and actors are sometimes on hand for a discussion with the audience. Check the *City Weekend* guide for titles, dates and times.
Zhongri Qingnian Jiaoliu Zhongxin, 40 Liangmaqiao (2km/1¼ miles east of the Kempinski Hotel).

Huguang Guildhall (Beijing opera)
One of the capital's must-see events, Beijing opera is the quintessential Chinese theatre. The Guildhall has been hosting performances since 1807. Of the dozens of venues offering this historical musical theatre, this is the most atmospheric.
3 Hufangqiao, Xuanwu District.
Tel: (010) 6351 8284.
Metro: Fiepingmen.

Sanwei Shuwu (Sanwei Bookstore) (Traditional music)
Traditional Chinese music performed by some of Beijing's best classical musicians in a rustic teashop and bookstore. Friday is Jazz Night, and on Saturday evenings musicians play traditional Chinese instruments such as the *pipa* and the *guzheng*.
60 Fuxingmennei, Xicheng District.
Tel: (010) 6601 3204.
Fri–Sat performances 8.30–10.30pm.
Metro: Xidan.

Weibishi (Vibes Nightclub)
The nightclub scene is constantly changing in Beijing, but Vibes has been rocking around the clock for years. Top DJs spin hip-hop, house, Latin-jazz and more at this trendy little lounge.
4 Jiuxianqiao, Chaoyang District.
Tel: (010) 6437 8082.
Metro: Chaoyangmen.

Zhongshan Gongyuan Yinyue Tang (Forbidden City Concert Hall)
This very regal concert hall has superb acoustics and comfortably seats up to 1,400. If your timing is right, you might be treated to a performance by the Beijing Symphony Orchestra or the China Philharmonic. The *City Weekend* guide carries reviews of the most recent performances.
Zhongshan Gongyuan, Xichang'an Jie, Xicheng District.
Tel: (010) 6559 8285.
Metro: Tiananmen Xi.

Sport and leisure

Chinese Culture Club (Tai Chi)
Inspired by the grace of the octogenarians in the park? If you want to learn this ancient martial art, enrol for a few classes at the Culture Club.
29 Liangmaqiao, Chaoyang District.
Tel: (010) 6432 9341.
www.chinesecultureclub.org. Metro: Dongzhimen.

Cycle China
Rent bicycles to join the thousands of Beijingers who throng the streets every day on pushbikes. The city is completely flat and most main roads have

cycle lanes. Or join a five-day cycling tour along the Great Wall of China.
12 Jingshan, Dongcheng District (across the street from the East Gate of Jingshan Gongyuan). Tel: (010) 6402 5653. www.cyclechina.com. Metro: Tiananmen Xi.

Equuleus International Riding Club (Horseback riding)
Equestrian club that accepts non-members.
Sun He, Chaoyang District. Tel: (010) 6432 4947. Metro: Dongzhimen.

Le Cool (Ice skating)
There are several outdoor rinks in the winter months, but otherwise head over to the underground shopping centre that connects China World Hotel and Traders Hotel and you'll find this enormous indoor rink. Skate rental available.
Guomao Liubing, 1 Jianguomenwai. Tel: (010) 6505 5776. Open: Sun–Fri 10am–10pm, Sat 10am–midnight. Metro: Guomao.

BEIJING ENVIRONS

Changcheng (The Great Wall)

Accommodation

Red Capital Ranch ★★★
If you want a room with a view of the Great Wall, then this Manchurian hunting lodge is perfect. The ten suites have stone walls and quaint wood carvings. The lodge is ideally located for walks in the nearby countryside.
28 Xiaguandi Village, Yanxi Township, Huairou. Tel: (010) 8401 8886. Email: info@redcapitalclub.com.cn. www.redcapitalclub.com.cn

Fragrant Hills Park

Accommodation

Fragrant Hills Hotel ★★
Beautifully located in the middle of the park from which it takes its name, this hotel was designed by architect I M Pei in 1983 and, although somewhat rundown nowadays, it is still a splendid and relaxing place to stay northwest of the city. The outdoor swimming pool is delightful, but crowded at weekends.
Fragrant Hills Park, Haidan District. Tel: (010) 6259 1166. Fax: (010) 6259 1762.

Ming Tombs

Sport and leisure

Beijing International Golf Club
Nestled alongside the Ming Tomb Reservoir, this meticulous golf course now hosts major competitions. A challenging 72-par course. Caddies provided.
Changping (46km/29 miles north of Beijing). Tel: (010) 6076 2288. Open: 7am–7pm.

Miyun County

Sport and leisure

Nanshan Ski Resort
Open from November to March, this is China's top ski resort. The ten ski runs are carefully sculpted. Ski lifts, ski rental, restaurants and bars all make for a fun winter's day out.
Shengshuitui Village, 40km (25 miles) north of Beijing Airport. Tel: (010) 8909 1909. www.nanshanski.com

Tianjin

Accommodation

Lishunde Dafandian (Astor Hotel) ★★
Built in 1863 by the British, the Astor has hosted China's 'Last Emperor', Pu Yi, as well as Sun Yatsen and the US President Herbert Hoover. The period furniture of the lobby alone lends a wonderful old-world ambience.
33 Tai'erzhuang.
Tel: (022) 2331 1688.

Hyatt Hotel ★★★★★
The Hyatt offers everything a 5-star hotel should, and it's perfectly located in the centre of the city. Rooms are tastefully furnished and the luxurious bathrooms are just what's needed after a hard day's slog around Tianjin's streets. Famed for its Xiang Wei Zhai Dumpling Restaurant, the hotel also boasts Cantonese, Japanese and Western restaurants. Unusual facilities include a riverside jogging track.
219 Jiefang Bei Lu.
Tel: (022) 2330 1234. www.tianjin.regency.hyatt.com

Eating out

Goubuli Baozidian (Goubuli Stuffed Bun) ★★
The Goubuli dates back over 100 years and is rightly famous for its *baozi* (steamed buns) filled with pork, chicken or shrimp. With 98 different types of buns and dumplings there is no shortage of choice.
77 Shandong Lu.
Tel (022) 2730 2540.
Open 7.30am–10pm.

Entertainment

Cosy Cafe and Bar
This busy, well-patronised establishment is popular with locals and expatriates, and throbs nightly to the sound of live music. The place can be very crowded late in the evening and the dance floor can get pretty wild.
68 Changde Dao, Heping.
Tel: (022) 2312 6616.
Open: 5.30pm–1.30am.

NORTH OF BEIJING

Chengde

Accommodation

Mountain Villa Hotel ★★–★★★
Located directly opposite the Bishu Shanzhuang (Imperial Summer Villa), this hotel is exceptionally good value. With a variety of rooms to suit all tastes and budgets, six restaurants, a shopping centre and business facilities, it is the best option in Chengde. The rooms in the main building are much better than the slightly cheaper rooms in the smaller building at the back.
127 Xiaonanmen Lu.
Tel: (0314) 202 3501.
www. hemvhotel.com/english

Yunshan Hotel ★★★★
Chengde's top hotel, the 4-star Yunshan, is not an attractive building, but the rooms are spacious, comfortable and, above all, quiet. A tour-group favourite, the hotel is locally noted for its first-class Cantonese restaurant.
2 Banbishan.
Tel: (0314) 205 5888.
Fax: (0314) 205 5885.
Email: webmaster@cdyunshan.com

Eating out

Jiuyuan ★★
A spacious restaurant visited mainly by tour

groups, the Jiuyuan serves some very good local cuisine. The *lurou* (grilled deer) in a piquant sauce and the *cong shao yezhurou* (wild boar with onions) are excellent. Also try the homemade Jiuyuan sausages. Be prepared for some exotic oddities on the menu.
22 Wulie Lu.
Tel: (0314) 202 2227.
Open: 11am–10.30pm.

Dalian

Accommodation

Gloria Plaza Hotel Dalian ★★
Business-oriented hotel with good facilities for families. There is everything here from a swimming pool and gym to a barber shop and disco. Located in the heart of the city.
5 Yide, Zhongshan District.
Tel: (0411) 8280 8855.
Fax: (0411) 8280 8533.
Email: gloria@gphdalian.com.
www.gphdalian.com

Hotel Nikko Dalian ★★★
Formerly known as the Oriental Palace, this spectacularly situated hotel overlooking Dalian's harbour and just a short stroll from famous Zhongshan Square offers first-rate accommodation. Facilities include an indoor swimming pool, tennis court, solarium, Jacuzzi and sauna. All rooms include satellite TV, internet access, mini-bar and particularly beautiful bathrooms.
123 Changjiang Lu.
Tel: (0411) 8252 9999.
Fax: (0411) 8252 9900.
www.jalhotels.com

Shangri-La Dalian ★★★★
This huge hotel has traditionally furnished, relaxing rooms and it's in a good location for exploring central Dalian. All rooms offer wireless internet access, mini-bar and large bathrooms. An indoor swimming pool and gym are on-site to work off the extra calories accumulated from Dalian's many food stalls serving high-calorie treats.
66 Renmin Lu.
Tel: (0411) 8252 5000.
Fax: (0411) 8252 5050.
www.shangri-la.com

Eating out

Wanbao Seafood Restaurant ★★
When in Dalian, eat seafood! There are currently two Wanbao restaurants in the city centre and there may be more by the time you read this, such is the popularity of Wanbao. The Labour Park address is the more opulent of the two (the other restaurant is in Zhongshan District, near the Hilton Hotel). The seafood is divine: try the stir-fried prawns, the steamed scallops, sea bream and abalone.
108 Jiefang (near Labour Park), Zhongshan District.
Tel: (0411) 8881 2888.
Open: 10.30am–10pm.

Entertainment

Laohutan Jidi Haiyang Dongwuguan (Polar Aquarium)
This is one of a number of attractions at Laohutan Leyuan (Tiger Beach Park). The aquarium is home to a number of species from both the North and South poles including polar bears, walruses,

seals, beluga whales and penguins. Dolphins perform several times a day and for children there is a section where it is possible to interact with a variety of different marine creatures.
Laohutan Leyuan (Tiger Beach Park). Tel: (0411) 8289 3111. Open: 8am–6pm. Admission charge.

Sport and leisure

Dalian Shide (Football)
The football (soccer) season runs from March to November and Dalian Shide FC are the undisputed kings of the Chinese league. If there is a game on while you are there, you can pay on entry at the 56,000-seater stadium. Great atmosphere.
Dalian People's Stadium. www.shidefc.com/english

Laohu Tan (Tiger Beach)
The top spot for sunbathing, swimming, natural scenery and family entertainment. Check out Seabed World, Bird Sing Wood and the Polar Region Museum, which hosts a splendid dolphin show.
4 km (2½ miles) southeast of the city centre. Free admission; attractions moderately priced. Bus Nos 30 & 712 from Zhongshan Square.

Harbin

Accommodation

Holiday Inn ★★
With its excellent location near the heart of Harbin's historical Daoliqu area and Sheng Suofeiya Jiaotang (St Sophia Cathedral), the Holiday Inn offers good value. Facilities include a gym, sauna, massage rooms and snooker table. Guest rooms are spacious and attractively furnished with satellite TV and mini-bar.
90 Jingwei. Tel: (0451) 8422 6666. Fax: (0451) 8422 1661. www.ichotelsgroup.com

Songhuajiang Gloria Inn Harbin ★★
Located at the crossroads of historical Zhongyang Dajie (Central Avenue) and Sidalin Gongyuan (Stalin Park), this large hotel is perfectly located for both summer and winter visitors. Its façade perfectly matches Central Avenue's other Russian architectural masterpieces. Its unpretentious rooms are comfortable, but basic. The Boathouse Restaurant serves good seafood dishes, while the Western/Chinese breakfast buffet is not bad for the price.
257 Zhongyang Dajie. Tel: (0451) 8463 8855. Fax: (0451) 8463 8533. www.giharbin.com

Harbin Romantic Hotel ★★★
This 3-star hotel is a sound choice for budget travellers looking for Western amenities at cheaper prices. It's only a few minutes' walk from the city's main walking street and St Sophia's Church. The heated indoor swimming pool is a splendid bonus.
178 Shangzhi, Daoli District. Tel: (0451) 8677 5555.

Eating out

French Bakery ★★
If you have ventured this far in northeastern China, then you'll probably be ready for a good cappuccino and some croissants. A full

coffee menu, assorted pastries and ice cream are written up every morning on the chalkboard menu.
174–185 Zhongyang.
Tel: (0451) 8911 3753.
Open: 8am–10pm.

Shenyang

Accommodation

Liaoning Hotel ★★
Built in 1927 by the Japanese and superbly renovated in 2001, the Liaoning is all marble staircases, period furniture and beautiful tiled floors. It's certainly one of the most atmospheric hotels in the Northeast. All rooms have towering ceilings and tasteful furnishings. Other facilities include a tennis court and sauna.
97 Zhongshan Lu.
Tel: (024) 2383 9166.

Traders Hotel ★★★
Beautifully designed, the Traders includes its own large shopping arcade and is well situated for most of Shenyang's major sights. From the sumptuous lobby to the large comfortable rooms, the hotel oozes style. Amenities include internet access in all rooms, steam room, fitness centre and some fine restaurants, including the famed Shang Palace.
68 Zhonghua Lu.
Tel: (024) 2341 2288.
Fax: (024) 2341 1988.
www.shangri-la.com

Eating out

Meiahli Korean BBQ ★★
A large number of Koreans live in Shenyang and that means good Korean restaurants. Meiahli's specialities include cold boiled noodles (*lengmian*), which might not sound too tempting, but are actually very tasty with a plate of *kimchi* (Korean pickles) and a bottle of local beer. Other standards include barbecued beef and a fruity tea (*zaocha*).
62 Kunming.
Tel: (024) 8341 5547.
Open: 10am–9pm.

SOUTH OF BEIJING

Datong

Accommodation

Datong Hotel ★★★★
Renovated in 2000, this 4-star hotel offers large, classy rooms, many of which have balconies overlooking the extensive landscaped gardens. Recreational facilities are excellent, including tennis courts and a snooker room.
37 Yingbin Xi.
Tel: (0352) 586 8111.
Fax: (0352) 586 8100.
www.datonghotel.com

Eating out

Tongheyuan Hotpot ★
Huddle around the pot and cook your own meal. An especially good way to keep warm on a cold winter night. You dip meats, vegetables and bean curd in a steaming broth, and wash it all down with cold local beer.
Chezhan Qian Jie, beside the Feitian Hotel.
Tel: (0352) 280 3111.
Open: 11am–9.30pm.

Dengfeng

Accommodation

Shaolin International Hotel ★★★
The best and most convenient rest stop when visiting Shaolin is this 3-star hotel in Dengfeng. The neat rooms are suitable for

foreign tourists with air conditioning, mini-bar and satellite TV, and the hotel even offers lessons in kung fu.
16 Shaolin.
Tel: (0371) 6286 6188.

Jinan

Accommodation

Crowne Plaza Jinan ★★★★★
As is to be expected from the Crowne Plaza group, this fine 5-star hotel is the best in town. Situated next to Chuan Cheng Guangchang (Spring City Square), Jinan's attractive heart, most of the city's major sights are just a short drive away. Each large, attractively furnished room boasts a broadband internet connection. Other hotel amenities include an indoor swimming pool, sauna and whirlpool.
3 Tianditan.
Tel: (0531) 8602 9999.
Fax: (0531) 8602 3333.
www.ichotelsgroup.com

Kaifeng

Accommodation

Kaifeng Guest Hotel ★★
Good value for money. This tourist-friendly hotel is comfortable, but not luxurious. Rooms have the full range of amenities and the hotel also has a fitness centre, swimming pool, spa, tennis courts and bowling.
66 Middle Ziyou.
Tel: (0378) 595 5589.
Fax: (0378) 595 3086.

Dongjing Hotel ★★★
Near the bus station, the Dongjing is situated inside Kaifeng's ancient southern walls. A reasonably quiet 3-star option, the hotel is set in its own garden and boasts a range of facilities, including a small shopping centre, beauty salon and a friendly karaoke lounge.
99 Yingbin.
Tel: (0378) 398 9388.
Fax: (0378) 595 6661.

Eating out

Shao'e Huang Restaurant ★★
An elegant restaurant that is always busy. A wide selection of meat, fish and vegetable dishes is displayed for you to choose from. Don't forget to try Kaifeng's famous *wuxiang shaobing* (five-spice bread), which, like pitta, can be opened and filled.
214 Zhongshan.
No phone.

Luoyang

Accommodation

Atravis Executive Hotel ★★
Opened in May 2007, this is a business-oriented hotel that is central, clean and has polite English-speaking staff.
19 Tianjin, Jianxi District.
Tel: (0379) 6468 3888.

Peony Hotel ★★★
An above-average Chinese high-rise 3-star hotel located close to Luoyang's Wangcheng Gongyuan (Peony Park) and its peony exhibition centre. Most rooms are quite large and attractively decorated, but like many Chinese hotels there is little in the way of facilities.
15 Zhongzhou Xi.
Tel/Fax: (0379) 6468 0000.

Pingyao

Accommodation

Dejuyuan Hotel ★
Pingyao is famous for its lovely folk-style guesthouses with their distinctive Qing-era

courtyards, and the Dejuyuan is one of the finest. Centrally located and directly opposite China's first ever bank, the hotel is also rightly famous for its excellent Shanxi dishes.
43 Xi.
Tel: (0354) 568 5266.
Fax: (0354) 568 5366.
www.pydjy.net

Tian Yuan Kui Guesthouse ★
A delightfully modest courtyard hotel designed with Ming and Qing architecture and décor, this is a favourite place for younger travellers. Located right in the middle of the Old City. Great value for money.
73 Nan.
Tel: (0354) 568 0069.
Fax: (0354) 568 3052.
www.pytyk.com

Qingdao

Accommodation

Oceanwide Elite Hotel ★★★★
Location is the essence of this excellent 4-star hotel, overlooking Qingdao Bay and the attractive Zhanqiao Pier. Though a fairly new hotel, it's built in colonial style, fitting in perfectly with Qingdao's old German legacy. A first-class restaurant, good business facilities, and well-maintained, spacious rooms make this a fine place to relax.
29 Taiping.
Tel (0532) 8299 6699.
Fax: (0532) 8289 1388.
www.oweh.com

Eating out

Qingdao Cuisine Restaurant ★★
Unsurprisingly, Qingdao cuisine involves lots of seafood. This restaurant is located on the first floor of the Huiquan Dynasty Hotel. Crab dishes and mussels are always delicious, but for something more exotic try the shark's fin soup and the braised sea cucumber with minced pork.
Huiquan Dynasty Hotel, 6 Nanhai.
Tel: (0532) 8299 9888.

Qufu

Accommodation

Mingya Xintan Hotel ★★
The imposing, modern concrete façade hides the friendly service and unique Chinese style found inside this simple, 2-star hotel. Although a little out of place in the ancient atmosphere of Confucius' birthplace, this budget hotel is a welcome combination of modern convenience and antique Chinese décor.
36 Datong Lu.
Tel (0537) 319 7888.

Taihuai

Accommodation

Yinhai Shanzhuang ★★
Built in Qing style, this hotel looks like a mountain temple in Wutai Shan. Popular with tour groups, south-facing rooms have lovely mountain views.
Xiao Nanpo Cun, opposite Nanchan Si.
Tel: (0350) 654 3676.
Fax: (0350) 654 2949.

WEST OF BEIJING

Lanzhou

Accommodation

Lanzhou Legend Hotel ★★★★
Located in the heart of the city, this four-star hotel has excellent restaurants, a health centre and a nightclub. The suites are comfortable and are decorated with original

Chinese paintings inspired by the 'Flying Celestials' murals found in the Dunhuang Grottoes.
529 Tianshui.
Tel: (0931) 853 2888.
Fax: (0931) 853 23333.
Email: legend@lanzhoulegendhotel.com.
www.lanzhoulegendhotel.com

Eating out

Mingde Gong ★★
Lanzhou is rightly famous as the centre for the unique Gansu school of cooking. This large restaurant serves an astonishing variety of these Gansu dishes, including the famous *jincheng baita*, an unusual assortment of cold meats designed to look like the city's famous Baita (White Pagoda). The *niurou chaomian* (beef noodles), known locally as *Lanzhou lamian* (Lanzhou beef noodles), are highly recommended.
191 Jiuquan.
Tel: (0931) 466 8588.
Open: 10am–2pm & 4.30pm–10pm.

Xian

Accommodation

Xian Shuyuan Youth Hostel ★
A cute courtyard residence, this youth hostel is ideal for those who prefer a jolly ambience and meeting people to the sureties of hot water and air conditioning. Friendly staff can help organise itineraries and offer tips. There are also kitchen facilities and bike rental.
Nan Dajie Xi Shun Cheng Xiang 2A.
Tel: (029) 8728 7720.
Fax: (029) 8728 7720.

Bell Tower Hotel ★★
Located right in the heart of the city, this hotel is managed by the Holiday Inn group and facilities are modern and comfortable. The view of the Bell Tower in the square opposite at sunset can be quite breathtaking. Note that the Bell Tower Hotel is not the same as the Bell and Drum Tower Hotel across the road.
110 Nan.
Tel: (029) 8760 0000.

May First Hotel ★★
A good location and an inexpensive option. With a bustling lobby and a popular restaurant, May First always appears busy. In 2007 the hotel underwent much-needed renovations.
351 Dong.
Tel: (029) 8721 2212.
Fax: (029) 8721 3824.
www.may-first.com

Howard Johnson Ginwa Plaza Hotel Xian ★★★
For those who like that little extra in luxury, this is an elaborate hotel with splendid and immaculate suites. Ask for a room on a high floor to enjoy a vista over the ancient South Gate. A lavish breakfast buffet awaits you in the morning.
18 West Section, Huancheng Nan Lu.
Tel: (029) 8842 1111.
www.hojochina.com

Hyatt Regency Xian ★★★★★
Well situated within the walls of the old city, this superb 5-star hotel attracts many tour groups. The grand interior and the high standards of service make the Hyatt a delight. Amenities include a fitness club, tennis court,

spa and pizzeria. All rooms include wireless internet access.
158 Dong.
Tel: (029) 8769 1234.
Fax: (029) 8769 6799.
Email: reservation.hrxian@hyattint.com.
www.xian.regency.hyatt.com

Eating out

Defachang Dumpling Restaurant ★★
Established in 1936, this enormous restaurant is a city landmark. Located between the Bell and Drum Towers, it offers over 100 different choices of *jiaozi* (pasta-wrapped dumplings). Try the famed Dumpling Feast for a *jiaozi* banquet with fillings including savoury chive, duck, fish, shrimp and even sweet walnut marzipan. A hotpot and an impressive number of appetisers and cold salads will come with your meal. Be careful: ordering *à la carte* can be much pricier.
Zhonggulou, 1 Xi.
Tel: (029) 8727 6021/ (029) 8721 8260.
Open: 10am–midnight.

Laosunjia ★★
Excellent family-run Muslim restaurant. Try the house speciality, *yangrou tang* (mutton soup), and the rich *yangrou paomo* (meat stew with glass noodles). Be prepared for a down-to-earth 'point at what you want' approach to service. Local beer washes it all down and can make for a fun night.
364 Dong, Beilin District.
Tel: (029) 8721 4438.
Open: 11.30am–2pm & 5pm–9pm.

Qujiangchun Restaurant ★★
Apparently founded in 1912 by Li Qinsi, who used to cook for the empress dowager of the Qing Dynasty. The restaurant now mainly serves dishes based on Tang Dynasty royal recipes. Waiters dress in period costume.
192 Jiefang.
Tel: (029) 8744 2439.
Open: 11am–10.30pm.

Shang Palace ★★★
This grand restaurant specialises in Cantonese delicacies along with a number of classic Chinese seafood dishes. Choose from abalone, shark's fin, bird's nest soup and many other exotic dishes. Imported wines also available.
8 Chang Le Xi.
Tel: (029) 8322 1199.
Open: 11.30am–2pm & 5.30pm–10pm.

Entertainment

Didi's (Nightclub)
Xian is renowned for nightlife and Didi's is the place that really rocks, especially at weekends. Very popular with the younger crowd. The DJ usually alternates with a live singer. Loud music, but not too pricey. Foreigners often get in free!
Huangcheng Xi Lu.
Open: 8pm–midnight.

Tang Dynasty Theatre
Set meals, fusion cuisine and a lively Las Vegas style show are the themes here. Exotic names such as 'Heart of the Dragon' (crispy king prawns) and 'Willow's Melody' (taro and water chestnut dessert) accompany a colourful and creative 90-minute floorshow. A Cantonese lunch buffet is also available.

A schedule of show times is available on the theatre's website. Expect to pay 200 RMB per person for the show and a good meal.
75 Chang An.
Tel: (029) 8782 2222.
www.xiantangdynasty.com.
Open: 9am–11.30pm.

Xian Diwang Club (Nightclub)
The Xian Diwang Club is the most exclusive nightspot in town. Good variety of music, cocktails and a more refined atmosphere than most other clubs.
Zhuque.
Tel: (029) 8522 7569.
Open: 8pm–midnight.

Xian Huxian Farmer Painting Gallery
This fascinating art gallery, displaying thousands of paintings by local artists from the Huxian County area to the southwest of Xian city, features some excellent folk-art paintings. Apart from permanent displays, the gallery has an exhibition about the history of the paintings and a section where guests can try their hand at imitating the method.
No 17 Building of Kaiyuan Group Corp of Jitong University, East Development Zone.
Tel: (029) 8268 3330.
www.peasantspainting.com. Open: 8.30am–5.30pm. Admission charge.

Xian Qujiang Haiyang Shi Jie Haiyangguan (Xian Qujiang Ocean World)
A great place to take children, Ocean World combines entertainment and education. Highlights include an underwater tunnel where you can watch sharks and rays swim around and above you, a dolphin show, a rainforest exhibition, and an interactive area where children can handle various creatures.
5 Yannan Yi Lu.
Tel: (029) 8553 3555.
www.xianoceanworld.com.
Open: 9am–6pm.
Admission charge.

GETTING AWAY FROM IT ALL

Dunhuang

Accommodation

Silk Road Dunhuang Hotel ★★★
In an incredible location at the edge of the sand dunes south of Dunhuang, the hotel looks like an old Han fortress. Rooms are tastefully decorated in warm desert colours. Some guest rooms even mimic the traditional Silk Road caravanserai-style of accommodation. The Dunhuang provides every possible convenience, including sand sledding and camel riding on the adjacent dunes.
Dunyue.
Tel: (0937) 888 2088.
Fax: (0937) 888 2086.
www.the-silk-road.com

Eating out

Feng Yi Ting ★★
With the striking red lanterns hanging from the ceiling and the large dining hall, the Feng Yi Ting (Chamber of Grandeur) certainly lives up to its name. The excellent Cantonese and Sichuan specials also go a long way to making this particular dining experience well worthwhile. Traditional dancers present nightly performances in the courtyard next to the restaurant in the

summer months between July and September.
Silk Road Dunhuang Hotel, Dunyue.
Tel: (0937) 888 2088.
Open: 7am–11pm.

Kashgar

Accommodation

Chini Bagh Hotel ★★
A rather sprawling, unattractive place, built on the grounds of the old British Consulate. There's a wide choice of rooms in three separate buildings including some pretty basic dormitory accommodation. The rooms in the International wing are spacious and comfortable, and here you'll find a very helpful travel agency. It can arrange trips and transportation to all the surrounding sights.
144 Seman.
Tel: (0998) 298 0671.

Eating out

Lao Chayuan Jiudian ★★
A fine Uighur restaurant serving some of the region's very best dishes, including lamb shish kebabs, beef noodle soup and *polo* (a Uighur rice speciality). For local residents this is the place to eat. Dishes are attractively presented, which makes a change from the rather unattractive approach of most restaurants in this part of the world.
251 Renmin Xi.
Tel: (0998) 282 4467.
Open: 10am–11.30pm.

Turpan

Accommodation

Grand Turpan Hotel ★–★★
The Grand, renovated in 2001 and with a new wing added, is one of the best options in town. Rooms are generally quite large and airy, and all have satellite TV and a mini-bar. The hotel also runs a rather good Muslim restaurant. The tour desk in the entrance hall provides valuable information on local tours.
20 Gaochang Lu.
Tel: (0995) 855 3868.

Urumqi

Accommodation

Hoi Tak Hotel ★★★★★
Urumqi's premier lodgings, this centrally located 36-storey monolith is a genuine 5-star hotel, a claim not always truthful in China. Rooms on the upper floors provide breathtaking views of the nearby Tian Shan (Heavenly Mountains). Facilities include an indoor swimming pool, snooker tables, sauna and whirlpool. Most unusually, there's also an eight-lane bowling alley.
1 Dong Feng.
Tel: (0991) 232 2828.
Fax: (0991) 232 1818.
www.hoitakhotel.com

Entertainment

Fubar
This popular venue shows regular live football from the English Premier League, Spanish Primera Liga and Italian Serie A. In season you'll also be able to catch up on other major world sporting events. The pizza is first class and there's a great selection of foreign beers and cocktails. They also run a good book exchange.
Gongyuan Bei.
Tel: (0991) 584 4498.
Open: 10am–midnight.

Index

A
accommodation 132–5
camping 134
home stays 134
hotels 132–5
pilgrims' inns 135
air travel 128, 150
amusement parks 80
Ancient Culture Street, Tianjin 59–60
Ancient Observatory, Beijing 34–5
antiques 145
Aquarium, Beijing 161
Aquarium, Dalian 165–6
architecture 15
art galleries 143, 172
Astor Hotel, Tianjin 60
ATMs 151

B
Badaling 5, 67–8
Baima Si 91
Bangchuidao Scenic Area 80
Banpo Neolithic Village Museum, Xian 110
Baotu Quan 98
bars and pubs 141–2
Beidaihe 72–3
Beihai Park, Beijing 36–7, 40
Beijing 5, 6, 21, 22–3, 26–51, 126
accommodation 158–9
bike tour 40–1
children's entertainment 148–9
eating out 159–61
entertainment 140, 141–3, 161–3
public transport 130–1
shopping 144–5
sights 26–49
sport and leisure 162–3
Beijing environs
directory 163–4
sights 52–3, 56–65
Beijing Zoo 37, 161
Bell and Drum Towers, Beijing 39
Bell and Drum Towers, Xian 111, 112, 116
Big Wild Goose Pagoda, Xian 111, 113
bike tour, Beijing 40–1
Binyang Caves 94
Bird Island 122
Biyun Si 52
Black Tiger Spring 98
Bodhisattva Peak 90
Bronze Temple, Taihuai 90
Buddhism 17

C
calligraphy 14
camping 134
car hire 130–1
caves
Ancestor Worshipping Cave 94
Binyang Caves 94
Damo Cave 96
Longmen Caves 25, 93–5
Mogao Caves 25
Ten Thousand Buddha Cave 94
Yungang Caves 21, 24, 85–6
Changbai Shan 72, 122–3
Changcheng (Great Wall) 5, 21, 66–71, 82
Changchun 73–4
Chengde 21, 23, 74–5, 78–9, 164–5
Chiang Kai Shek 12, 91–2, 116
China Great Wall Museum, Badaling 68
China Puppet Theatre 148
Chinese medicine 54–5
Chinese opera 15, 32–3, 140, 143, 162
cinema 15, 143, 162
circus 33
Cixi, Dowager Empress 9–10, 52, 53, 62, 63, 64–5
Coal Hill, Beijing 38
Confucian Temple, Qufu 101
Confucianism 16
Confucius 8, 16, 101
conversion table 153
counterfeit goods 145
Cow Street Mosque, Beijing 28–9
credit cards 133, 137, 150–1
crime 134, 156–7
Cultural Revolution 10–11, 12–13, 89
customs regulations 150
cycling 131, 162–3
Beijing bike tour 40–1

D
Dabei Monastery, Tianjin 59
Dailuo Peak 90
Dalian 79–80, 165
Daming Lake 98
Datong 24, 84–6, 167
debit cards 151
Deng Xiaoping 11, 13
Dengfeng 96, 167–8
Diamond Throne Pagoda, Beijing 52
disabilities, travellers with 153
Donghai Park, Dalian 80
Dongshan 94
drinking water 133, 156
Dunhuang 25, 86, 172–3

E
Eastern Qin tombs 52–3
eating out 136–9
Beijing cuisine 137–8
Cantonese cuisine 138
Sichuan cuisine 138–9
vegetarian food 138
wines, beers and spirits 100–1, 139
Ejin Horo Qi 121
electricity 133–4, 150
embassies 157
emergencies 156–7
emergency telephone numbers 156
entertainment 140–3
environmental problems 4, 76–7, 127
ethnic minorities 80, 110, 123
etiquette 14, 136–7
Ever-White Mountain Nature Reserve 72, 122–3

F
feng shui 15
Five Springs Park 107
Five Terrace Mountain 87, 90–1
food and drink 136–9
football 147, 166
Forbidden City, Beijing 21, 41, 42–7, 51
Forest of Pagodas, Denfeng 96
Forest of Stone Stelae, Xian 112
Fragrant Hills Park 61–2, 163

G
Gansu 6
Gaochang 124, 125
Genghis Khan Mausoleum 121
golf 146–7, 163
Grand Canal 104–5
Great Bell Temple, Beijing 37–8
Great Hall of the People, Beijing 49
Great Leap Forward 10, 12
Great Mosque, Hohhot 121
Great Mosque, Xian 110–11, 112
Great Wall 5, 21, 66–71, 82
Guizhou 54

H
Hailaer 121
Hanging Temple Datong 84–5
Harbin 80–2, 166–7
health 156
Heaven Lake 75, 122, 125
Heavenly Mountain 125
Henan Province 91–5
history 8–11
Hohhot 121
home stays 134
horseback riding 163
hotels 132–5
Houhai Lake, Beijing 40
Huang He 6, 91–2
Huanghua Cheng 69
Huaqing Hot Springs 116
Huayan Monastery, Datong 84
Hui people 110
hutongs, Beijing 24, 26, 38, 41

I
Ice Lantern Festival 18, 81, 82
ice skating 163
Id Kah Mosque, Kashgar 123
imperial court 50–1
Imperial Palace, Shenyang 83
Imperial Summer Resort, Chengde 21, 74–5, 78
Inner Mongolia 6, 120–1
Inner Mongolia Museum, Hohhot 121
insurance 156
internet access 150
inventions, Chinese 114–15

J
Japanese Germ Warfare Experimental Base 82
Jet Spring 98
Jiaohe 124–5
Jinan 97–9, 168
Jinshanling 71
Juyongguan 69

K
Kaifeng 92–3, 168
Karakoram Highway 124
Karakul Lake 124
Kashgar 25, 123–4, 173
kite flying 147, 148, 149
Kong Family Mansion, Qufu 101

L
Lama Temple, Beijing 35–6
Lanzhou 106–7, 127, 169–70
Long March 10, 118–19
Longbao Black-Necked Crane Sanctuary 122
Longmen Caves 25, 93–5
lost property 157
Luohou Temple, Taihuai 90
Luoyang 95, 168

M
malaria 156
Manchuria 6, 72
Mao Zedong 10–11, 12–13, 88, 118–19
Mao Zedong Memorial Hall, Beijing 41, 49
Marble Boat, Beijing 64
markets 144–5
martial arts 146
medical services 156
Ming Tombs 57–8
Mogao Caves 25
monasteries
Dabei Monastery, Tianjin 59
Huayan Monastery, Datong 84

money 150–1
Monument to the People's Heroes, Beijing 47–8
museums
 Banpo Neolithic Village Museum, Xian 110
 China Great Wall Museum, Badaling 68
 Dalian Modern Museum 79
 Gansu Provincial Museum, Lanzhou 106–7
 Inner Mongolia Museum, Hohhot 121
 Luoyang Municipal Museum 95
 Museum of Natural History, Beijing 31
 National Art Museum of China, Beijing 36
 Palace Museum of the Last Emperor Pu Yi, Changchun 74
 Qin Terracotta Army Museum, Xian 116–17
 Rishengchang Financial House Museum, Pingyao 87
 Shaanxi Historial Museum, Xian 111
 Shandong Provincial Museum, Jinan 99
 World of Tsingtao, Qingdao 101
 Xinjiang Autonomous Region Museum, Urumqi 125
music
 Chinese opera 15, 32–3, 140, 143, 162
 classical 14–15, 141, 162
Mutianyu 71

N
Nanshan Ski Resort 163
Nanshan Temple, Taihuai 90
National Art Museum of China, Beijing 36
National Theatre, Beijing 141, 142
newspapers and magazines 152
Nine Dragons Screen, Datong 84
north of Beijing
 directory 164–7
 sights 72–83

O
Old Summer Palace, Beijing 39
Olympic Games 2008 13, 146
opening hours 151
Opium Wars 57

P
Palace Museum of the Last Emperor Pu Yi, Changchun 74
Palace of Prince Gong, Beijing 38
passports and visas 151
Peking Man 58
pharmacies 151–2
pilgrims' inns 135
Pingfang 82
Pingyao 21, 86–7, 168–9
Polar Aquarium, Dalian 165–6
police 157
pollution 4, 127
Polo, Marco 9, 108–9
postal services 152
Prime Minister's Temple, Kaifeng 92–3
Pu Yi, Emperor 10, 56, 60, 73–4
public holidays 152
public transport 128–31
 air travel 128, 150
 buses 131
 train services 129–30, 150
Putouzongcheng Temple, Chengde 78–9

Q
Qianfo Shan 99
Qianmen District, Beijing 29
Qin Terracotta Army Museum, Xian 116–17
Qing Dong Ling 52–3
Qing Xi Ling 56
Qingdao 21, 25, 100–3, 169
Qinghai 6, 122
Qinghai Lake 122
Qufu 101, 169

R
religion 16–17
Rishengchang Financial House Museum, Pingyao 87

S
safety 134, 156–7
St Sophia Cathedral, Harbin 81
service charges 137, 152
Shaanxi Historial Museum, Xian 111
Shandong Province 97–103
Shandong Provincial Museum, Jinan 99
Shanhaiguan 82
Shanshgaangan Guild Hall, Kaifeng 93
Shanxi Province 84–7, 90–1
Shaolin Temple, Dengfeng 96
Shenyang 82–3, 167
Shipton's Arch 124
Shisan Ling 57–8
Siberian Tiger Park 81
Silk Road 25, 109, 123
Simatai 71
skiing 163
Small Wild Goose Pagoda, Xian 111, 113
smoking etiquette 152
Song Shan Scenic Area 95–6
Sony Explora-Science Centre 148
Sonyang Academy 96–7
south of Beijing
 directory 167–9
 sights 84–103
sport and leisure 146–7
Summer Palace, Beijing 21, 62–5
Sun Asia Ocean World 80
Sun Island Park, Harbin 82
Sun Yatsen Memorial 52
sustainable tourism 152

T
tai chi 147, 162
Taihuai 24, 87, 90, 169
Taoism 16–17
taxis 130–1
Tayuan Temple, Taihuai 90
teahouses 142–3
telephones 152–3
Temple of Heaven Park, Beijing 41
temples
 Bronze Temple, Taihuai 90
 Confucian Temple, Qufu 101
 Confucius Temple, Beijing 35
 Eastern Peak Temple, Beijing 34
 Five Pagoda Temple, Hohhot 121
 Great Bell Temple, Beijing 37–8
 Hanging Temple Datong 84–5
 Lama Temple, Beijing 35–6
 Luohou Temple, Taihuai 90
 Nanshan Temple, Taihuai 90
 Prime Minister's Temple, Kaifeng 92–3
 Putouzongcheng Temple, Chengde 78–9
 Shaolin Temple, Dengfeng 96
 Tanzhe Temple, Beijing 58
 Tayuan Temple, Taihuai 90
 Temple of Azure Clouds, Beijing 52
 Temple of the Flourishing State, Jinan 99
 Temple of Heaven, Beijing 21, 29–31
 Temple of the Reclining Buddha, Tianjin 61
 Temple of the Source of Buddhist Teaching, Beijing 27–8
 Temple of the White Cloud, Beijing 27
 Tianhou Temple, Tianjin 60–1
 White Horse Temple, Baima Si 91
 Yungang Cave Temples 85–6
 Zhongyue Temple, Dengfeng 97
Terracotta Army 21, 23–4, 116–17
Thousand Buddha Mountain 99
Tian Chi 72, 122
Tiananmen Square, Beijing 13, 41, 47–9
Tianhou Temple, Tianjin 60–1
Tianjin 59, 164
Tiger Beach Ocean Park 80, 166–7
time zone 153
tipping 137
toilets 153
Tomb of Confucius 101
tombs
 Eastern Qing tombs 52–3
 Ming Tombs 57–8
 Shenyang 82–3
 Tomb of Qin Shi Huang Di 117
 Western Qing Tombs 56
train services 129–30, 150
Turpan 25, 124–5, 173
Turpan Depression 124
Tushuk Tash 124

U
Uighur people 123
Urumqi 125, 173

V
vaccinations 156

W
Wangfujing Street, Beijing 35
west of Beijing 106–17
 directory 169–72
 sights 106–17
Western Qing Tombs 56
White Pagoda Hill, Lanzhou 106
World of Tsingtao, Qingdao 101
Wutai Shan 21, 24, 87, 90–1

X
Xian 6, 23–4, 107, 110–13, 116–17, 170–2
Xian Huxian Farmer Painting Gallery 172
Xian Qujiang Ocean World 172
Xihai Lake, Beijing 40
Xikai Cathedral, Tianjin 61
Xining 122
Xinjiang 6, 123
Xinjiang Autonomous Region 106
Xinjiang Autonomous Region Museum, Urumqi 125

Y
Yellow River 6, 91–2
Yungang Caves 21, 24, 85–6

Z
Zhengyici Beijing Opera Theatre 29
Zhongyue Temple, Dengfeng 97
zoos 37, 148–9, 161

Acknowledgements

Thomas Cook Publishing wishes to thank the following libraries and associations for their assistance in the preparation of this book.

All pictures were supplied by DAVID HENLEY/CPA MEDIA with the exception of:

DREAMSTIME (1, 56, 58, 59, 80, 86, 90, 92, 93, 98, 110, 111, 117, 124, 125, 127, 131, 142, 149)

BRENT MADISON (78, 79)

WORLD PICTURES/PHOTOSHOT (87, 91, 94, 96)

For CAMBRIDGE PUBLISHING MANAGEMENT LTD:

Project editor: Diane Teillol

Copy editor: Joanne Osborn

Typesetter: Trevor Double, Paul Queripel

Proofreader: Karolin Thomas

Indexer: Marie Lorimer

SEND YOUR THOUGHTS TO BOOKS@THOMASCOOK.COM

We're committed to providing the very best up-to-date information in our travel guides and constantly strive to make them as useful as they can be. You can help us to improve future editions by letting us have your feedback. If you've made a wonderful discovery on your travels that we don't already feature, if you'd like to inform us about recent changes to anything that we do include, or if you simply want to let us know your thoughts about this guidebook and how we can make it even better – we'd love to hear from you.

Send us ideas, discoveries and recommendations today and then look out for your valuable input in the next edition of this title.

Emails to the above address, or letters to Travellers Series Editor, Thomas Cook Publishing, PO Box 227, Unit 9, Coningsby Road, Peterborough PE3 8SB, UK.

Please don't forget to let us know which title your feedback refers to!